These

Words

Tom Bennett

Lovstad Publishing
Poynette, Wisconsin
Lovstadpublishing@live.com

ISBN: 0615766196
ISBN-13: 978-0615766195

Printed in the United States of America

These

Words

These Words

These words, these very letters here
Upon this very page appear
A tribute to my lowly pen
Which serves me time and time again.

But only words of truth and good
Are good enough, I really should
Be clear on that important fact
If hearing them we choose to act.

And so my pen is charged with hope
To show respect and help us cope
To always write with some good cheer
Upon these very pages here.

Tom Bennett

These Words

Introduction

I write my own introduction because I can't trust anyone else to convey exactly what I have tried to do with this book. Ultimately, it is about honesty. I have always seen myself as a pragmatic, fairly average human being who tends to "cut to the quick" most of the time. Unfortunately, I am also somewhat creative and artistic—which means that although I usually say what I mean, I often "colorize" things a bit to make myself appear much more intelligent and interesting to others—than I actually am. This is all about that.

I have a little trouble with book covers. Often enough, the picture—if there is one—is totally unrelated to what the book is about and is designed to attract attention. It's a marketing thing. The title is usually an esoteric, artsy phrase that means nothing until you have read the book—either that or some kind of clever play on words. I am neither creative enough nor clever enough to get away with these conventions. I, therefore, decided to just do what I do IN the book—ON the book. Oh, some might say, "That's different," or "That's clever," but actually I realized it was an easy way to have a unique book cover without having to think very much... my kind of book cover.

...as for the rest of the book...

It is a compilation of several unrelated writings: poems that come out of nowhere and which likely will end up in the same place, a few short stories with few redeeming qualities, and an assortment of... uh... commentaries or observations that will leave you longing for less. It is a book of such pointless purpose and failed direction that there is truly no justifiable reason to continue reading beyond this page. If you have inexplicably chosen to venture beyond the cover and are, at this very time, reading these very words, then you are obviously accepting the fact that your taste and investment in literature leaves much to be desired. Read on then at your own risk. You have been warned.

An excerpt from an unfinished autobiography...

I was born with a black strike right off. My name, Gordon Bennett, (which can be found in the Oxford Dictionary) I have heard, is used in England as an exclamation of surprise and disgust—much the same as our American, "Oh shit!" Although I do not believe in omens, I can't help but think that this is an unfortunate way to begin a life of potential greatness. But fortunately for me, I have been ignorantly unaware of this prophetic British euphemism for most of my life, and was not burdened with this semantic knowledge until the ripe old age of forty seven. The disappointing English meaning of my name, however, does indeed describe, with uncanny clarity, the character of my life, nonetheless.

...and as a side note...

Upon learning that my name had unfortunate characteristics, I decided around 2007 that something must be done about it. I, therefore, did a search on the internet for the address of Buckingham Palace in London. I then drafted a letter to the queen of England to notify her of my situation and to suggest a "diplomatic" solution to my problem. I decided that at some point in my future, I would likely visit England as a vacation destination—and with the mere utterance of my name, would undoubtedly suffer humiliation at the hands of the English citizenry— especially in pubs. It seemed only natural, then, to request a "voucher" for one pint of English beer—good in any pub I might find myself in by happenstance; a reasonable request in my estimation. The request, however, was denied in a letter that I received about a month later. The person who apparently screens the queen's mail in Buckingham Palace informed me that they (the palace folks, I guess) receive far too many similar requests to single out an occasional recipient for favoritism. They apologetically declined my request.

Later, after I had lost the letter, I realized that even the rejection letter from Buckingham Palace might have been enough to negotiate a free pint here or there. But, alas, the letter is gone, and although I will certainly travel to England someday, I have resigned myself to brave the ridicule and, no doubt, pay for my beers.

Stopping
(10-21-96)
I am constantly on the go
Running and running
I really should just stop
For a while—just stop
And keep stopping
Until I can't stop anymore
Then I'll stop stopping
And go again

This Real Morning
(10-22-99)
This real morning—clothed in wonder
Illumination with no end
No such words as pain and hunger
No regrets or fears to mend
All directions undirected
Possibilities alight
See your twenty—raise another
Guts and glory to the night

This real morning—like no other
Born upon a hope of gold
No one really understanding
Noticing, or finally sold
All appreciate beginnings
Holding temporary hands
When tomorrow's disappointment
Soon enough gets up and stands

Although these first writings speak of beginnings, it should not be assumed that a chronological account of my life will follow. I am prone to written ramblings and odd little explorations beyond a path that really doesn't exist. Just as a puzzle is made up of many, many little unique pieces that somehow fit together to make a coherent picture, these separate writings likely will do the same. If there is a good reason for someone to have a curiosity about my life, I am at a complete loss to understand it. I do, however, have a certain love for the art of written expression which hopefully will be worth a reader's perusal.

How Old Am I
(11-16-94)

How old am I, a friend inquired
Fortyish or so, I said
Not so young to sprint a mile
But not so old I'm nearly dead

And had I come along much sooner
I would be much older now
Now that's a worthwhile revelation
Really sounds like me somehow

But anyway, as I was saying
And I am being honest here
I could have been some twelve months older
Had I not been late a year

So much of what I see or experience somehow finds its way onto my pages. One spring day, while wandering about behind my garage, I simply looked up and in a moment between moments heard a robin's distinctive call.

The Things Above
(11-21-94)

A robin is singing, high and sweet
With little robins under feet
Whose open mouths implore to eat
A bug or worm or other treat

And down below I'm in my chair
Relaxing with an eye up there
And getting just a bit of air
Before I have to be somewhere

I think I'm fortunate to know
That I can stop before I go
And contemplate a minute or so
The things above I sit below

I am convinced that I should have been born in the late eighteen hundreds. It was a time of rhyme and what I call entertainment poems. Although there were certainly exceptions, a great deal of the poetry was meant for easy enjoyment, pure and simple. And though there are always those who just have to dig for deep meanings and hidden messages and soul-searing emotion, I absolutely loathe esoteric riddly poetry that has to be figured out. What's the point? It is written to be read, isn't it? It is meant to be a personal expression that is set down for others to ponder, right? Well alright, I'm a pragmatic sort of person. I usually just like to pass on a bit of what makes a certain thought special, a sudden moment memorable, or a unique taste tasty. If a reader of my writings chooses to look for deep or hidden meanings that are not readily apparent, he/she is making it all up. I'm not that smart, and I'm certainly not that clever, and I don't really like that sort of thing. Really.

The Special Morning
(12-5-94)

A big golden morning has come up today
To brighten and heighten this fine winter day
But though driving to work is a daily routine
It's special this morning for what I have seen

For off to my left there's a man in a car
Who is keeping my pace and going as far
He drives just like me but in black silhouette
I guess that's as close as a shadow can get

But then something happened that I thought was nice
It captured the moment, to be more precise
I used to think shadows were lifeless and black
But when I smiled and waved, my shadow waived back

There was a time when I did a lot of driving. I decided late in my life that if my wife was industrious enough to work for a living and take college classes on the side, as well as orchestrate a home life—I could too. I enrolled, therefore, in the local university and discovered to my great surprise that some of the mundane, but required, courses (like English, for example) were actually quite interesting. Whereas I grew up believing that poetry was a singular waste of a "normal" person's time, I found that I became increasingly inspired to write it—especially while driving.

The Bird
(2-1-95)

Somewhere back behind the seat
I think I have a parakeet
Who only seems to come alive
Whenever I begin to drive
It could be just a squeaky door
Or something loose beneath the floor
But when I stop to trace the sound
It's always nowhere to be found
I guess I need a helper then
To crawl back there and look again
But this time I will drive along
And trick my little bird to song
And after, if my plan is good
I'll dab a finger underhood
And then, by God, I'll have some peace
And feed my little bird some grease

The Coon
(11-10-94)

I came upon a coon last night
As I was driving home
Lying there as dead as nails
In broken glass and chrome

He probably just wandered out
In front of someone's car
And maybe just to get a snack
But never made it far

I wonder if the other coons
Will even know he's gone
But even if they do, I guess
They'll have to just go on

The Place
(12-12-94)

There's a place along the way
I travel past most every day
An old abandoned farmhouse there
Has lately gone beyond repair

Windows staring blank and sad
Forget the happy life it had
Peeling paint and sagging porch
Are begging for the fireman's torch

But what if it should come to that?
This place I'm always staring at
Could have some possibilities
A fine new house, a few new trees

The land is good, the well is fine
Maybe it could all be mine
Tomorrow, as I'm driving past
I won't be going quite so fast

The Drive
(2-10-98)
Trees, from standing, now come running
Endless asphalt slips easily under and away behind
Though it is closer than it appears, fading
My eyes rattle guardrail posts like a stick on pickets
I see the old cans in the brown grass ditch
While red-winged blackbirds dip a wing from the fence
The wheel agrees with my hands
The world ahead somehow parts and I go through
When I stop, it hesitates
When I go, it parts and I go through again
The drive is between the start and the end

    As I stated earlier, most of my ideas are simple ones. Although I have been told otherwise, I do not consider myself to be a thinker of deep thoughts. I don't even like deep thoughts—they take too long. They aren't easy. I may very well be wrong, but I find most people who think deeply to be either boring or condescending—or vice versa.

The Robins Are Back
(4-17-95)

The robins are back, the robins are back
The fat little buggers are on the attack
Hundreds of thousands of worms will be lost
For robins all know when we've had our last frost
All sorts of insects and bugs on alert
Are doomed to be dinner and likely desert
So many critters will soon be a snack
Since Spring has come early and the robins are back

A Dollar
(10-24-95)

A dollar gambled, lost or spent
Is one one wonders where it went
And saved it could have soon become
A couple with the interest from

Lest someone mistake me for a shallow, lazy writer of drivel, a few pieces of a more "thoughtful" persuasion might be in order. Let not the size of a poem determine its value. The value of a poem comes from an appreciation of how close to home it hits, how heartfelt emotion is conveyed, and whether someone can even understand it.

An excerpt from an essay about love...

Like pains of pleasure, or light misty rain
Like chronic chocolate ice cream on the brain
It writhes like silk against a window's night
And brings down giants despite their might
This thing of legends, this fruit of hearts
It comes in whispers then loud departs

What a bunch of crap. At least, that's what I would normally tend to say, but my little impromptu poem turned out too good to just dismiss it with a casual heartless comment like that. So I'll try to explain myself instead. Love is real. It can be wonderful or a terrible burden, but if there is one thing I have found to be true about love, it is that it is like a little cloud that envelopes you. You can't get a hold of it. You can't wave it off. Sometimes, you can't even see it—but you can feel it. It's what I call "an intangible." Do you feel tired sometimes? Can you hold "tiredness" in your hand? No. Do you feel happy—maybe even giggly like when someone tells you a good joke? Sure you do, but can you hold "happiness" in your hand—or bottle it and sell it? No. So what CAN you do with love? Nothing. You can't keep it from creeping in to your life. You can't shut it off when it does. You can't measure it. You can't even convince anyone that you have it very well. Great—just great!

So what's going on here? Why do things like this seem to be intangible, unattainable, unmeasureable, elusive lofty things that are real, but beyond our understanding? I don't know. Don't ask me. I'm just trying to tell you what I DO know. I know love is in my heart and mind. I don't know why, but it is. I know love is goofy and intangible and sometimes on-again, off-again. I know that everyone has at least some of it somewhere inside them. I know that it is worthwhile and desirable and it can be "catchy." I also know that I haven't told you anything you didn't already know somehow inherently. I guess, in the interests of being somewhat constructive, I can try to give my best advice about how to handle love. Just live it. Embrace the good stuff and let the rest go. Exercise restraint and respect where appropriate and love with abandon when you think you safely can. That's it. Go for it.

The Words
(10-31-95)

The words are simple, pure and true
I keep them in my heart for you
And know you have a matching set
That gives me more than others get

And even to my final day
The words are yours for me to say
And never will I break the vow
I swear in earnest here and now

And so the words are keenly kept
For you they're given to accept
And guarded well by honor bound
They're yours forever safe and sound

Comfy Old Sweater
(10-6-95)

It goes without saying, It's right there to see
And nothing or no one can take it from me
A feeling I wear like a comfy old sweater
And little-by-little it gets better and better

I guess that it's normal to harbor some doubt
But I don't have any to worry about
I know when I'm hungry, I know when I'm tired
And I know that my wife is both loved and desired

The Moment
(3-25-95)

It's easy to know when the feeling is right
It's there like a fire to light up the night
It's subtle and fleeting, yet strong as an ox
But it's not everyday opportunity knocks

So stand up in front of admiring friends
And watch for the moment when loneliness ends
Somewhere between all the pomp and the prayer
For one fleeting second some magic is there

Remember the moment above all the rest
There won't be another one better than best
Keep it forever, familiar and new
And prove that you mean it by saying, "I do."

Morning
(4-12-96)

Oh, how right the morning fair
For lovers wakened everywhere
By unintended dream-filled touch
The warm new sun or birds and such
To smile a moment eye to eye
Before the daily cares come by
To pull them cruelly from their beds
While love still freshly fills their heads

17

My Heart
(4-6-96)

My heart, it seems, is not just flesh
A beating muscle in my chest
But something more, outside myself
I set upon my highest shelf
And save forever, through and through
My greatest gift reserved for you

The Rest Of Our Lives
(11-13-06)

The glass is nearly full these days
And problems are simply opportunities
I look up instead of down, forward instead of back
By choice, and of my own free will

I see the girl in the short dress of flowers
Standing in the spotlight among the others
Calling me from inside somewhere
While not seeing me at all

I no longer see you with my eyes alone
The fleeting glimpses of how it should be
Are like permanent freshly washed windows
That show me everything every day in color

It's all so clear, having been there and back
And it's easy to choose where I want to be
And I can, you know, and so can you
Just in time for the rest of our lives

A life is never chronicled in a neat and well-defined way, devoid of deviations from a pre-determined path or only including the planned and expected things we count significant enough to list. It is, instead, a mess of bits and pieces, good and bad, big and small. That, when laid down into words, seems hardly interesting or worthy of the memory retention of others. It is, therefore, likely that most life stories are presented not only in the interest of sharing one's esoteric tales of a life lived well or not, but as likely for the vanity of the writer—whether or not the life exposed is his or hers or not. There is a certain satisfaction derived from the artistic presentation of such a life, assuming that the endeavor is successful in its intentions. Being looked upon as an author or a poet or simply a "writer" has an appeal to the vanity, despite the questionable virtue of having it. Be that as it may, there is also the invisible force that seems to make us express ourselves—whether appreciated or not. That force is where my interest lies. It is both a reason and an excuse. It is intangible, but recognized by every writer—or artist—or expresser of one thing or another. It is one of those peculiarly "human" characteristics that distinguish a creative person from an industrious ant.

One of my bits or pieces involves an innate and

incessant interest in astronomy—and by default, astrophysics. I have been known to rail on for hours about gravity and its place in the universe. When explained in a "plain-language" way as it relates to the structure of the universe—or at the very least, the solar system, it transforms from being a boring and vague force that makes apples fall to earth to one of the fundamental forces of nature that provides an understanding of why the moon revolves around the earth—and why the earth revolves around the sun—and what exactly the sun is, and why.

The Stars

The stars are really something—so distant and so bright
And oh, so much a part of every single night
Like little hints of hope in a dark and endless black
That wait for some discoverer to travel there and back

Sixteen On Twelve Fourteen Ten
(12-14-10)
Oh, it's not like me to brave the crispy dark
and noiseless cold
Pretending I'm not getting old
and calling it my morning walk
While others driving by will talk
about the weird and crazy guy
Who's always looking at the sky it seems—
so strange at six o'clock

But there I was all bundled up
and heading down the driveway though
Three miles I always try to go
before I start my normal day
If someone knows a better way
to lose a pound or two or three
I'll gladly listen if it's free
and doesn't hit me like a rock

December means the Geminids are back
and putting on a special show
For those who have the guts to know
the value of a sleepless night
When one more hour surely might
be better in a warm and cozy bed
But no, I'm freezing like a fool instead—
and not a hint of morning yet

I turned out on the county road
amazed at Venus nearly overhead
So brightly lit I might have said
it was a savior star or UFO
And hardly just a planet though
it was impressive nonetheless
The average person wouldn't guess
it isn't easy to forget

And then a silent silver streak
went arcing eastward in a flash
Like glitter in a frenzied dash
across the deep and endless sky
And only some sad fool would try
to capture it in lowly words
That won't sit still like winter birds
at feeding time—that simply wouldn't do

A half a mile and several more,
and then another grand surprise
Came poking eastward for my eyes
to rest upon for a brief spell
And I could very easily tell
the ISS had come to call
With sun-reflected light for all
to see who braved the weather for a view

Another meteor came and went
as I came to where I turn around
And start back home—
the sound of morning laying hints
of orange and purple dawn
With eyes aloft I continued on,
a long streak here, a short one there
And despite the cold I couldn't care less
about the coming of a routine day

I turned back into my driveway then
and knew I would remember when
On December fourteen of twenty ten
I counted sixteen falling stars
At least seven passing cars—
and one international space station flew by
It's enough to make a grown man cry—
but otherwise nothing much happened

The Harvest
(12-15-93)

When the moonrise falls on the soft new snow
And sparkles there like a diamond throw
People come and people go
But I would have to stop there though

And think about the stars that night
That fell upon this very site
It's funny, now, to think I might
Have come and gone for wrong or right

And missed it all, and never known
A moment I can call my own
I stopped there though, and though alone
I reaped the harvest that was sown

Underneath A Waxing Gibbous
(11-11-94)

Underneath a waxing gibbous
On this clear November night
Little towns in each direction
Twinkle with their distant light

Fields of moonlit hope and promise
Having kept their bargains well
Roll away in subtle darkness
Asleep—as far as I can tell

And even though I feel the evening
Cold against my hands and face
It's underneath this waxing gibbous
I have found this perfect place

Three Quarter Moon
(11-21-94)

A three quarter moon is rising and yellow
A welcome companion for one tired fellow
Mile after mile through the long dreary night
But now I can see by the three quarter light
I almost feel warmer or somehow more mellow
Just knowing the moon is there three quarters bright

I sometimes find that my most intriguing thoughts arrange themselves best when I am busy doing unrelated things—like driving, or working. I can be called a hypocrite, I guess, because I have more than once complained of the young female drivers who pass the slower me with a cell phone glued to their heads—when I am guilty of physically writing ideas, poems or songs down on a notebook—when I should have been looking at the road. One day at work, when I should have been working, I was inspired to relate the weird but true story of a client's visit to my office.

The Craigs
(4-11-95)

"Arlo's blind," his daughter said
And there he sat with eyes ahead
And Hazel hollered at his ear
'Cause Arlo also couldn't hear

A tall and sagging nice old guy
He liked to look you near the eye
And bellow questions loud and clear
Though I was sitting very near

And Hazel didn't mind at all
A wife above and beyond the call
Helping Arlo day and night
As hearing aid and proxy sight

I didn't know his daughter's name
Or even really why she came
Hazel seemed to manage well
As far a Arlo and I could tell

So there we were, the Craigs and me
All shouting loudly as can be
And then when all was said and done
We all got hoarse... the cost of fun

The Little Light
(10-8-95)

There's a very small and fragile light
Which hanging from my mirror tonight
Is comfort in this evening hour
Despite it's waning candlepower

And even though its light is dim
It stands against the dark and grim
A friend to keep me company
When home is where I ought to be

And finally, when its power dies
I'll drive between the fireflies
That line the highway up ahead
And lead me to my home and bed

And lying in my bed of dreams
I'll think about how nice it seems
To always have a little light
To click before I say goodnight

An excerpt from another book that I almost wrote...

     I think I look at our world a little differently than most people. Whether I'm right or not is just another point of contention, I guess, but I see our world as an ever-changing place that has seen the coming and going of many species and probably will for a long, long time—which is a very short, short time in the incredibly long timeframe and huge scale of the universe. We, the people of earth, seem to me to be just another species that evolved from nearly nothing, have flourished for a while, and who will one day die away—just like countless other species in the earth's 4.5 billion year history. I see us (people) as something akin to beavers. We sort of move in to an area, cut down a bunch of trees and build a big pile of debris to live under for a while---until some flood wipes it out and forces us to move somewhere else where we get in a fight and get killed or driven out again. Are beavers natural? Yes. Is their pile of debris with all the unused junk lying around natural? Yes. Is the flood that messes it all up natural? Yes. How about the fight with another beaver? Yes. Is there anything that ISN'T natural about beavers? Not that I know. Ok, so what about us? Are we natural? Yes. Is our pile of debris natural? Well, everything we build on this earth comes from the earth... Yes. Is the pollution we leave behind natural? Well, everything we leave behind came from the environment—whether we transformed it into some other form or not. So are we really mistreating the environment? Probably not—it's all natural causes and effects and will, in the entire scheme of things, work itself out in a natural way. Yeah but what if it means we choke ourselves out of a nice habitable place—that ain't natural, is it? Yes.

There's a real difference between doing what is bad for the environment, and doing what is bad for US. We can call it what we want, though—it's all natural. If we make ourselves extinct, it's natural. If we release a lot of greenhouse gases into the atmosphere and change the very climate of the earth, it, too, is natural—maybe it isn't the way things would have gone if we hadn't intervened, but we do intervene. It's natural that we do it, and it's natural that we (and the earth) suffer the consequences. Remember, though, I'm not talking about what is right or wrong—that's all in our heads... naturally.

Now you might think, "What kind of science is this?" My reply is, "It's not science, it's what I think." This isn't a science book. This is my little private forum and you, the reader, are most welcome to write yours, as well.

I also wanted to say something about science & the universe because, as I said earlier, I happen to be an amateur astronomer, and as such, I am constantly looking at many things from the perspective of a small speck in an unimaginably huge cosmos. Many things just don't seem as important as they otherwise might have when viewed from this vantage point. You will, therefore, certainly encounter many instances where I appear to dismiss issues as ridiculous—that others (like you, maybe?) might feel very strongly about. Oh well. Just because you likely paid for this book doesn't mean you get an opinion.

The universe is still very much a major mystery, but there are many discoveries—especially recent ones—that make certain well-established ideas look... well... stupid. As an example, for centuries, it was thought that the earth was the center of the universe and that the heavens revolved around it. Anyone who thought otherwise, like Copernicus and Galileo, had to tread very carefully or find themselves sequestered in the company of rats in the downstairs apartment. Eventually, the authorities had to accept the realities of proven science. Sooner or later, so do we. If we don't happen to BELIEVE the science, that's ok. Sooner or later the proofs will prevail and those of us who cling to a faith-based reality will either be revealed as misguided—or we'll kill each other. It happens both ways—but proofs will prevail nonetheless. Now think about what I am saying here. I'm not saying that proofs that are BELIEVED will prevail. What we believe has nothing to do with whether something is proven or not. I'm talking about reality, not our perception of it. There are many things in life that I have thought about, but which have taken on new meaning due to my relatively new understanding of how the universe works. As an agnostic, though, and a somewhat open-minded person, I leave myself open to the POSSIBILITY that I CAN be wrong—about anything. That possibility means that there is room for proofs—despite what I might currently think. It's absolutely justified and admirable to have skepticism—and to expect proofs, but it is also important to ACCEPT things when the time comes—whether they happen to go against the current thinking or not. I like to think I can do that.

From The Heavens
(10-10-94)

I wonder, sometimes, about what is important
And how much things matter to people like me
It's easy to think I'm the only one thinking
But then I remember how dumb I can be

And all the concerns and the worries we dwell on
Are probably problems we let ourselves make
But what if we looked at ourselves from the heavens
Surely it usually is all a mistake

No one would care if my life was a good one
A hundred years after I finally died
Those that have said that our lives do have meaning
Maybe, just maybe, mistakenly lied

While in college, I had an occasion to study for a short time the writings of ancient Greece: Homer, Dante, etc. I have to say that I was more than a little disconcerted to find out that the level of intellectualism expressed by these people of the past was on par with the best writers of modern times. It was hard for me to accept, at first, that the human race has not evolved to a higher level of consciousness; a more sophisticated level of thinking. We seem to have simply discovered some new technologies and demonstrated a myriad of ways to be the same as we were then. So I decided to make an attempt to "regress" to a level of communicating that might fit in nicely with the writings of these ancient Greek poets and philosophers.

Although I had no monumental lessons to convey, no masterful accounts of great battles, not even an interesting tidbit of modern life worthy of the grand style. I managed though, with no small effort, to put down a few lines in the style of these literate past masters.

An Evening Epic
(2-20-96)

And then I, within whom silence dwelled:
"Here sit'st I, well sustained by prior indulgence,
Intent upon sweet repose in the execution of my due.
Heavy are my eyes as the thirsty leaf after rain.
Slow are muscles too long without precious rest.
The pale mistress of the night rises east and bids me
Lie down and succor my workday wounds
Before her nightly westward disappearance.
And I, with trials yet unmet and second wind waiting
Bow gladly to her will with the morrow in mind.
Time enough, I say, and there surely is
For it has been so for all these years."

The Wonder
(11-16-99)

The wonder of a light existence
Nestled in the mire somewhere
Across the hopes and dreams of such a simple one
The all-consuming consequences
Bravely carried everywhere
Make honor seem so possible when said and done

The wonder of potential---waiting
Illuminated from within
Searching for the seam from which it finally pours
Hold the need for celebrating
Reign the speculation in
Saving for the day we open all the doors

The wonder of complete fulfillment
Is easier to say than do
Pity, though, to anyone who never tries
Make the try a real commitment
See it as the thing to do
Greatness, the result, if wonder never dies

Anyone who has worked for any company anywhere will know that what we call "common sense" is not only not common, but might also be a figment of someone's imagination entirely. Corporate policies rarely coincide with employees expectations. The same is true in reverse. Corporate thinking, from an employee's point of view, is perplexing at best and often leads to inexplicable actions by everyone concerned, mandated inefficiencies and universal feelings of mistrust and ineptitude. Other than that, things run fairly well.

I have an obvious bias against corporate thinking which I am not ashamed of. It is both justified and understandable given the rampant evidence that can be found in nearly any company anywhere. Business executives, bosses, supervisors, or whatever, seldom think of their employees as irreplaceable assets or valuable human beings worthy of compassion and adequate compensation. All too often employees are simply expendable liabilities or simply business expenses. I would never, for a moment, believe that this dynamic is likely to improve, but what if...?

The Guy Who Died

None of us are likely to live beyond the end of our lives, and the time we spend living is representative of our personal choice to be a worthwhile member of society—or a worthless one. We don't automatically become one or the other—we choose our path, however ignorantly. Invariably, when we do well, we are appreciated and reap the benefits it can bring; and when we do badly, we are alienated and suffer consequences generally considered unpleasant. Most of us, however, are a little of both—which can somewhat confuse the issue.

A guy died the other day—and almost as if to punctuate what happened, he didn't show up for work the next day. His wife was somewhat uncomfortable about it, his co-workers were convinced something wasn't right, and the company expected a possible vacancy at his work station. Oh, the world continued to rotate and revolve as usual, and the company opened and operated and closed in its usual routine, but there was something just a bit different. It is almost as if one grain of salt somehow turned up missing in the shaker. No one saw it disappear. No one knew which grain it might have been exactly, and no one seemed to be able to measure the difference. Something just wasn't right.

The guy who sat at the front desk wearing the uniform, was completely clueless. Had he been a little more on-the-ball, he might have reported the inexplicable absence of the one employee who didn't come through showing his badge, but with the sudden rushing of fifteen hundred other workers into the building within the twenty or so minutes before start time, there came an understandable oversight in human inventory management. As far as the company was concerned, he was off the hook. It could have happened to anyone. There was no point in bringing it to his attention, and there was no point in making more of it than what was already there. It was decided that since no one seemed particularly sure of what to do, nothing would be done—and that is, therefore, exactly what they did.

Just past the front desk, a large L-shaped glossy walnut counter led to the elevators. The pleasant receptionist looked blankly through her glasses at the massive cloud of employees drifting in to work every morning—looking forward to the first coffee break in the employee lounge. You could smoke in there, and grab a cold ham & cheese sandwich out of the vending machine for 75 cents. Her job was to tell people who didn't know where they were going where to go. This is a job very much in demand and practiced daily by the vast majority of employees everywhere. Few actually get paid for it though, and even fewer get good at it. When the guy who died didn't come in for work, the receptionist obviously didn't notice because of the throngs of people converging on the elevators, but the oversight, itself, was quite noticeable—and alarming—so it was with the shrewd and canny mindfulness of top management that a decision was made to rectify a previously unaddressed problem.

When the guy who died didn't show up, the company discovered the quandary. There was a person to greet people who came into the building—and give them guidance, but there was no one to notice—or help—those who didn't come in. What a huge oversight. Why hadn't anyone realized before this—that there was probably a vast number of people who never came in at all? Something would have to be done. But no one could seriously expect an entirely new area of expertise to be dropped into the lap of the receptionist. This called for a new position to be considered. It would require a completely different approach and specialized training. The people in top management made a note to show some appreciation in a meaningful way to those who die in the future. Without their help, problems like this would not be brought out in the open and dealt with. Big thanks were in order to the guy who died.

Upstairs in what was called "the big room," color coded rows of 5-1/2' high cubicles extended the length of the building and comprised the main work area. Each cubicle measured 6' x 8' and included a nice corner desk, computer, filing cabinet, and hall tree. A comfortable roll-around chair was provided, and a clear plastic sheet protected the thin-but-classy carpeting that seemed to be one large piece—but probably wasn't. The cubicle walls were made of some kind of acoustical panels to isolate noise from the other cubicles. Invariably, the inside walls of the cubicles were lined with pictures of kids, wives, husbands, fish, dead deer, and the inevitable newspaper cartoon. There was no night and day in the big room. If the drapes along the walls were opened, the sun—or some other annoying light— would always seem to be in someone's eyes—adding distraction to the doldrums. So the drapes were kept closed and the big fluorescent lights were kept on continuously to compensate for the lack of light. It was better that way.

It was the supervisor of "green row" that eventually noticed the absence of the guy who died—but not right away. As any good office worker will know, the first order of business in anyone's work day is to visit with other co-workers who haven't as yet died. A secretary would have the coffee ready, and people would gravitate slowly from one cubicle to another catching up on all the happenings of the last sixteen hours. This is the American equivalent to the Japanese custom of grouping together for exercise before the start of work in order to clear our brains for the task at hand. It is an essential part of the work day that prepares each worker for the work that they are expected to do while at work.

Once the initial visiting period had passed, the supervisor of each row is encouraged to attend a meeting to catch up on all the happenings of the last sixteen hours. This meeting is necessary for management people to feel important and look professional while preparing them to make the workers do the work that they are expected to do while at work. The meetings almost always take at least a half hour—meetings always do—it's better that way.

After the meeting, the row supervisors make their rounds—that is, they walk slowly down the isle making sure the workers see them and acknowledge them with moderate surprise and practiced respect. A brief exchange of small talk makes everyone feel good and contributes to higher morale and productivity.

When the guy who died didn't show up for work, he left his cubicle disconcertingly vacant—and his work undone. This would not otherwise amount to an insurmountable problem, but it left the supervisor with some questions. Why does this cubicle appear to be unoccupied? How can the importance of the supervisory position be appreciated by someone who doesn't seem to be present? What constitutes an excused absence? Who can fill in for whoever isn't here? Would it be better to simply overlook the absence and move on to the morning break in the manager's lounge? You can get a cold ham and cheese sandwich there for 50 cents in the vending machine. It isn't difficult to see why the stress involved with daily decision-making in management positions necessitates substantial compensation packages. Only people with exceptional connections, and relatives in high offices, are likely to have what it takes to become successful at the top of the business pyramid. They are the beating heart of any company—and worth whatever cut in benefits the rank and file workers are presented with. It is because of people like the guy who died that challenges present themselves which separate the men from the boys (so to speak).

Most of the co-workers who worked near the guy who died decided that he had a good reason for not being there. He was, after all, gone. People are not gone for no reason—this was common knowledge, and so it was with a baffled silence that the people in green row accepted his absence. The supervisor realized with the same shrewd powers of deduction that the guy was almost certainly gone because he was not there. These things can be figured out if one puts some mind power into it. He was satisfied that, once again, his supervisory skills had problem-solved another corporate dilemma.

Throughout the day, however, the supervisor came to realize that even though the guy who died was gone, and despite his good reason for being gone, at least a portion of his work was probably not getting done. No one could be sure, of course, since there was no one in charge of measuring how much work was *not* being done—only how much was *being* done. A supervisor's job is to make sure a certain amount of work gets done. This is accomplished by being seen from time to time—and by wearing fairly formal attire. There simply was no mechanism in place to oversee how much was *not* getting accomplished. He made a mental note to discuss the problem with upper management—with a recommendation to create a new department. There would have to be a department head, and a staff big enough to justify the expense. It's better that way.

Once again, the supervisor surmised, the guy who died was responsible for the realization that a new department was needed. Had the guy been present that day, no one would have noticed that a certain amount of work was not being done—there was no one to oversee that discrepancy, and there was no one to assume responsibility for the reports and clerical records, the monthly expenses associated with the department, or the proper management of such a department. A savvy supervisor with the motivation to bring this need to the attention of upper management was undoubtedly going to be considered for future upward mobility. But a certain measure of respect from the rank and file is helpful, as well. Although not necessary or required, this respect can only be attained by the occasional recognition of merit by a supervisor. If the workers are given the impression that they are appreciated from time to time, they will be more productive and happy employees—or at least it can be assumed they are. The supervisor decided that a memo would be generated that would show considerable corporate appreciation for the administrative advances inspired by the guy who died. This declaration of gratitude would go a long way toward fostering the kind of respect every supervisor hopes to receive. There could also be another benefit from issuing the memo. If the rank and file workers plainly and publicly see how impressed upper management is with the innovations inspired by employees who die, there is every likelihood that others could be motivated to do likewise. It is a win-win situation.

At the end of the day, the clock at each end of the big room indicated that it was time for the shift change. Each worker began preparing for the end of their shift by putting their work away an hour or so before quitting—and starting what appeared to be an unorganized "milling around" time when they visited with one another before leaving for their respective homes. In reality, though, this was actually a highly refined time of closure that is crucial to the completion of a successful day of work. All managers are aware of this—and in order to set an example, it is quite common for management people to leave a couple of hours early. Rank and file workers, however, will customarily complete this closure exercise during the last hour or so of work time so as not to affect the number of hours necessary for a full paycheck. Salaried supervisors do not sacrifice their pay by leaving early; this is a phenomenon reserved for rank and file employees—that is why they are not supervisors themselves. It is better that way.

As the shift workers drifted from the elevators past the receptionist, they did not notice the framed memo on the wall which was put in a prominent place for all to see. Eventually, everyone would know of it by spreading talk during the pre-work visitation period or the rushed breakroom talk at lunch the next day. In a week or so, a new walnut desk would be installed near the current one leading to the elevators, and a pleasant woman would be assigned to it with duties that address the needs of those who do not enter the building—and who are not able to be helped by the current receptionist.

As for the guy who died, he would be remembered for a time as one who contributed much to the company. His wife would receive a copy of the memo commemorating his accomplishments. His co-workers would be inspired to follow in his footsteps—perhaps even elevating themselves to higher positions on the corporate ladder. His supervisor would be invited to play golf on Thursday afternoons, and would receive a significant bump in his Christmas bonus. The guy who died would have his story detailed in the orientation manual as an example for new employees, and although his world would continue to rotate and revolve as usual, despite his absence, he would be happy that he had played an important part in it before he died.

We are all destined to live and die. It is our contributions to society, however, whether given while alive or sometime later, that will ultimately determine how we are remembered by those who remain after us. These remembrances are crucial as life lessons for the younger people who will die someday. And as for those of us who have already died, a certain amount of responsibility for how we are remembered is in order. It's better that way.

There are times when a simple look at something, for an unusual moment, is somehow different than it normally would be. An artist knows instinctively to capture this esoteric and fleeting chance at originality. A poet makes a mental note for some future rhyme. A child greets an invisible friend and shares the experience with a precious secrecy. A nut thinks the aliens caused it.

This Old Tree
(10-6-94)

Well there it lies, so old and grey
On ground it overlooked each day
Tall and handsome, one might say
Until it finally passed away

It's leaves have left it's branches bare
With twisted fingers in the air
But all the seeds that once were there
Are neighbors now, and everywhere

And now this lifeless trunk I see
Is firewood for folks like me
And soon a fleeting memory
Is what will come of this old tree

Breaktime
(10-8-95)

It was only a very few minutes at best
I only had time for a very short rest
There were so many things that still had be done
And everyone knows that it's work before fun

And then it occurred to me—what could I lose
If I sat myself down and I took off my shoes
And leaned my head back for an afternoon nap
Forgetting the world with its clock and its crap

Sooner or later you get to a point
Where you just want to quit and walk out of that joint
But then I'd just look like a bum or a jerk
So I put on my shoes and I went back to work

The Fire
(10-13-95)

I think the sun went down tonight
And left a fire burning bright
Along the long and distant line
Where evening earth and sky combine

And little trees and barns still stand
Against the burning hell at hand
And scream in golden silhouette
That they'll be here tomorrow, yet

And then as quickly as it came
The fire cooled its fearful flame
The screaming orange and raging red
Are purple now and nearly dead

But then tomorrow's waning sky
Will see another sunset die
And I will once again admire
The spent horizon's silent fire

I have never really considered myself to be a "real" writer—or poet—or any other kind of literary figure. I essentially have nothing significant to say, nothing profound to expound, and certainly nothing that anyone might find worthy of quoting. My cutesy musings appeal, generally, only to those who don't wish to "push" their brains very much—people I can relate to... relatives, perhaps. But then again, there may be a few unfortunate souls out there who actually like a playful rhyme better than an angry cry for social justice—or a light bit of fun more than a plea for some sort of esoteric understanding. Despite the fact that the twentieth century occurred, there may still be a place in this world for an uplifting lilt, a modicum of mildness, or a positive thought.

The Fly
(9-15-96)

This damn fly is going to die
As soon as I can catch him
I'll wonder why I had to try
As soon as I dispatch him

Jersey Gloves
(12-20-95)

I really like my Jersey gloves
That cost a dollar at the store
But no one else I know will wear them
Even when the rest cost more

I have a pair of fancy mittens
Leather, with some fleece inside
And plenty warm if I should wear them
But I don't, I must confide

I also have a pair of white ones
Thick with big and bulky seams
But they don't fit well in my pockets
Though they're good for cold extremes

But I'll just wear my new brown Jerseys
Even though they quickly shrink
They're warm and comfy on the fingers
Still the best I have to think

The Owl
(11-12-94)

An owl is calling out his question
From his favorite shadow tree
He never seems to ever listen
When I reply, "It's only me."

He calls as if he hasn't seen me
Could it be that owls are blind
Maybe he just calls routinely
If that's the case, well I don't mind

The Hairball
(4-4-95)

The hairball is back after prowling all night
And looks like the loser of some hairball fight
Though tired and hungry and a sorry old sight
He'll howl at the door 'til I turn on the light

Then he'll drag through the kitchen his tail hanging low
While whimpering and wining and walking real slow
And straight to the food dish he'll certainly go
But I have to watch closely, he throws up, you know

Then on to the living room sneaking about
Looking for somewhere for sleeping, no doubt
If he gets on the bed, well, I'll just have to shout
Or maybe I'll simply just throw his ass out

Gambling Night
(7-3-95)

It's always been a fearful thought
To gamble more than I have got
So many people come to that
Both peon or aristocrat

But I've been lucky heretofore
For never having wanted more
Than anyone deserves to get
For having placed a risky bet

And so I put my dollar in
The one-armed bandit gave a spin
And blessed me with a modest win
I left and never went again

Leisure time is something I hold very dear. I have made it my life's work to become proficient at it. When I retire, I hope to be a master leisure engineer, with experience in the various leisure arts—like fishing, artwork, music, writing, eating and whatever else I'm not likely to earn a living at. With luck, and a marital reprieve, I may find a bit of peace in my life—despite my somewhat lacking existence.

My Friend
(10-5-94)
I could sit for hours on end
And feel my tired muscles mend
My day from work, I can't pretend
A much anticipated friend

And only time would interfere
With time well spent, so very dear
An hour there, an hour here
Is soon another precious year

So all day long, if up to me
I'll tell you how it's going to be
A book, a nap, a break for tea
And all is well with my friend and me

My Porch Swing
(11-7-94)

I hung a porch swing out in front
Though barely a successful stunt
It hangs by chains that creak and squeak
As if it almost wants to speak

And even though it's not the best
It's really nice to sit and rest
And swing my dangling feet around
In rhythm with the creaking sound

And blind to all the things I see
Go passing by in front of me
No one even knows I'm there
And I don't even really care

But sometimes they can hear the squeak
And whirl their heads to catch a peek
So maybe I should oil the thing
And listen to a quiet swing

But then my feet would dangle there
As if it were a normal chair
And I might even miss the tune
My porch swing makes each afternoon

The Evening
(6-12-95)

If I could reach into the air
And grasp a twilight hanging there
I'd pull it down and wrap myself
In quiet, peaceful evening wear

And all the crazy, stressful things
A normal, busy workday brings
Would have to wait on some back shelf
To be tomorrow's burdenings

And then I'd make myself, at last
Put all my worries in the past
And nurse my nature back to health
To live a little not so fast

My Ultralite
(5-9-96)

I brought my ultralite today
In case I find along the way
Some hardly noticed spring fed stream
As good as how they always seem
With gravel bottom, grassy sides
And ledges where the big one hides
And overgrown with underbrush
To fend off the relentless rush
Of those who take without a care
Who'd never brave the brambles there
This is just the kind of hole
That prompts a guy to bring his pole

Home is where the heart is. Home is where you hang your hat. Home is where you keep your remote controls. There's no place like home. If I really tried, I could make this go on and on until you finally decide that you have made a grave mistake in taking up this manuscript. Instead, I'll simply say that, for me, home is where I am most comfortable, and most welcome, and most likely to go after being somewhere else. In my own personal case, home is a place that I created—with no small contribution from my wife and her good taste. I designed the house. I decided the driveway should have a gentle S-curve in it. I built the exposed foundation walls and laid the stone walkways and built the decks. It was my wife's idea to restore the "tillable" part of our property to its original prairie state. We carved out a small garden and work together growing our own food that doesn't travel down a conveyor, doesn't come out of a can or plastic bag, doesn't contain MSG, and doesn't cost very much.

But there are other qualities about "home" that are a bit less tangible and open to interpretation. We all have our individual feelings about where and how we live, but my feelings seem to squirt out of me from time to time in ways that are sometimes more than a little... weird.

The Walk
(4-25-01)

We went for a walk where the bald field ahead
lay harvested of beans
And the rutted road rolled left and right
with tractor tracks our guide
Budded woods on either side
made the field long and narrow
Turkey tracked and whitetail hoofed

We saw the lab see much to see
with a zigzag, nose-first interest
That made us grin—dog treats on our mind
The Easter egg sky pushed puffs
of animal shapes slowly to the east
Turning into cars and smiling silhouettes

The distant faded valley fell closer to the beat of our steps
But hid behind the crew cut knoll with its unleafed hair
And we crossed the fence to the oak leaf carpeted wood
With it's curly-Q ferns and May apple fingers

A long forgotten wind threw gnarly gates in our way
That we ducked under and stepped over and pushed aside
An Indian mound writhed a wrinkle along the hilltop
Of lichen logs down and mushroom steps up

The sun led us west along the valley rim,
and down the narrow spine to the mossy outcrop
Where a temporarily treed coon watched
our temporary trespass patiently
The river below smiled up at us after a long day on the road
Not unlike the one in the bean field, rolling left and right

Below, the town lights winked awake
one-by-one in the distant valley
While our golden guide went home for the day
An imagined line of cars stopped and goed
at a green and red pinpoint
That couldn't make up its mind

Soon the minimag in my pocket warned us it was time to go
And our walking sticks pulled us back up the hill
past the dusky rim and curly-Q's
We went back again along the wrinkled ridge
to the fence and field
Then across the crunchy bean stems
to the farm road and home

Harmony
(5-30-02)

The sky hung over the land bluely
While the trees to the South and West
rolled under a green quilt
The watery waves swirled current across the prairie field
As the gently curved drive hosted killdeer and dandelions
The paths led to bluebirds and deer prints
And the spring sprung quietly from a new ravine
The log bridge was at home between two slopes
Of the cool wood and above the earth's tear of happiness
The old barbed fence walked slowly around the garden
Where peace and color grow wild all year
And the big house stands like the North Star
At the center of a skyfull of trusted friends
Foreign, but good, in a harmony of new and old
Black and white, never and forever

I am writing "these words" in January (...and, as it turns out, February, March and April). "The holidays" have passed, but having come from a family (yeah right) that stretched Christmas out as long as possible, my wife and I dismantled our Christmas tree only yesterday—well into the month. We like having the tree in the house. We like watching TV together by the light of the cheerful tree. We even use the tree lights to sort of signal each other a welcome home when one of us has been somewhere. It also gives us a chance to yell at the cat.

Christmas Lights
(12-6-94)

Just look at all the Christmas lights
There's more than other Christmas nights
For every single house I see
Is showing off a Christmas tree
And every window, roof and door
Is hung with wreathes and lights and more
Las Vegas never looked so bright
As my own little town tonight
But if it wasn't bright like this
It's something I would surely miss
So hang them off the chimney stack
Down the sides and 'round the back
Christmas lights on every lawn
The more the merrier—dusk till dawn

Winter's Night
(11-29-94)

A winter's dark and dreary night
Grey with flakes that once fell bright
Hovers silently and cold
Insisting that the year got old

Endless days and weeks are filled
With empty trees and flowers killed
Coated by the frigid frost
That can't remember summers lost

Christmas
(11-24-94)

A winter's dark and freezing night
With all its cold and dreary might
Is every year a happy sight
With Christmas decorations bright

We often dread the coming snow
But then we wish we had some, though
For Christmas soon would come and go
Unhappily without, you know

And so we have the bad and good
To feel the fire, we chop the wood
And if we all did all we could
Then Christmas would be all it should

And speaking of winter…

It is disconcertingly often that someone will ask, "Well, are you sick of winter yet?" …or, "Are you tired of all the snow yet?" These queries are fairly common, but I have never really understood why. This is Wisconsin. We live here. We CHOOSE to live here. When we get old and go south for the winter, we tell each other, "I miss the seasons"—and move back. Let's face it, despite what we say, we like it. If we didn't, we wouldn't live here—or would we? If we are dumb enough to live where we don't like it, and complain about it like someone else should fix it, it can probably be said that we need to reevaluate our presence of mind. In other words, we're nuts.

A King
(11-28-94)

A few small flakes have floated down
And placed upon my head a crown
Of priceless white and silver jewels
And making me a king of fools

For any fool would wear his hat
And not a crown that melts like that
And yes, although it looks so nice
It's only frozen flakes of ice

But yet there's still a part of me
A little like a king would be
So pleased to wear my crown of snow
If only for a moment, though

The Woods
(12-10-94)

Things have changed a bit today
The woods I know have gone away
And standing over in their place
Are trees of delicate coral lace
Every frozen branch and twig
A feather, or a powdered wig
Or pretzel which is coated white
Every piece a sweet delight
But as suddenly as this woods came
Tomorrow it will look the same
As yesterday, before the frost
The frosted one forever lost

Winter
(11-30-94)

Here it is December now
Our summer came and went somehow
The wind and ice and cold and snow
Are here to let my heat bill know

And icy fingers give us clue
That only boots and cap will do
And collars up around the chin
For anyone who can't stay in

And this is how it has to be
No matter how it seems to me
Winter always comes and goes
As did the summer, I suppose

Sometimes, thoughts just seem to fall out of the sky. This happens fairly often to those of us of the artistic persuasion—as anyone of that sort will tell you. I might be riding along in a car when all of a sudden an old rusty car appears in a pasture by the fence, and while I might have passed that same old car a hundred times, for some strange reason I noticed it this time. Or maybe I just happened to be outside when a small flock of birds settled into the tree up ahead—and although that has happened many times, this time it catches my attention and I lapse into a goofy bit of rhyme for a time. Or maybe an old cigar advertisement suddenly comes to life with a sad and silent plea for more than a passing notice.

The Rustbucket
(5-14-96)

The old rustbucket is parked for good
Having gone as far as any car could
What once was sleek and shiny and black
Has now been pulled forever back
Behind the old machinery shed
Where it's been long since left for dead
And rusty now, from head to toe
It sits without a place to go
And that's what's really hard to face
A ditch is now its resting place
Chickens drive it nowhere now
And in the passing lane a cow
Meanders by without a glance
Unmindful of the circumstance
That brought this fine old car to this
A pile of junk no one will miss

Fruits
(1-24-96)

The tree bears fruits this morning high
Upon its topmost bows they fly
And settle in a cluster there
Which overlooks the morning air

The leafless limbs do little more
Than hold them till again they soar
To land on other limbs nearby
Fruits once more to catch my eye

And then the little buggers flew
Together on a silent cue
And now the tree was really bare
And so returned my empty stare

The Wooden Indian
(12-21-94)

The Indian stood with his back to the wall
Sober and silent, observing us all
Telling us nothing, but making his point
That anything's better than guarding this joint
With old wooden feathers and cracks in his quill
And butternut features forever held still
It isn't befitting a man of such pride
To stand on display for cigars sold inside
And so when I see him next time at the door
I'll smile and greet him as though he were more
Because maybe it's true that he's carved from a tree
But he'll always be more than just lumber to me

Most true stories, even the ones that have been made up, have a bit of sadness in them. No one likes sadness; and no one would go out of his/her way to seek it out or savor it like a particularly tempting candy. Yet, somehow we tend to appreciate it when it accents the lessons we learn from some unexpected hardship or a deserved unpleasantness. The Dalai Lama says that the negativity of adversity can be turned into a positive thing when the lesson learned makes our life better in some way. In this way, sadness can actually be a good thing.

I don't like it when at the beginning of a movie a message scrolls across the screen that says, "Based on a true story." What does that mean? Is it true, or isn't it? And does the fact that the story is based on truth make it more believable, or more worthy of our attention, or more... anything? I don't get it. ...but maybe I do...

The following story is "based on a true story," but is not true. Wait, wait... I'll explain. The main character was a good friend of mine for many years in real life. He was a neighbor who did much of what is depicted in the following story—but not all of it. He really did love the Cubs. He really did stand on the corner. He really did ride his old Schwinn out of town looking for aluminum cans. Anyone who knew him, before he died a few years ago, would recognize him instantly upon reading the story. Hopefully, those people would also know that I liked and respected him quite a lot. This story, then, is more of a tribute than a fiction.

...to my old friend Bill...

Can Day

The faded Zenith sign hung perpendicular to the front of the old two-story building on main street. Its two big front windows faced east--displaying geraniums and African violets and some leafy green vines. The front door, between the windows, opened into what used to be the TV repair shop, and what now served as a storage place for memories. The faded gray asbestos slate siding on the outside hadn't been painted in a long time, and the galvanized roof needed a new coat of aluminum paint. On the south side of the building, a little shed filled with firewood waited for winter, with the old blue pickup parked nearby—seldom driven anymore. Under one of the picture windows out front, a small hand made wooden bench had never been sat on.

Most days, Ben could be seen standing on the corner underneath the Zenith sign that no longer lit up at night. He always stood there—right at the edge of the sidewalk, looking up and down Main Street as if waiting for some long expected day to come by, and pick him up, and whisk him away on one last adventure. He and his wife had lived in the back of the old TV repair shop for as long as anyone could remember. Transistors had come along at about the same time as his social security, and he was sort of forced into retirement by the new technology. Now he lived only to live; getting up with the sun, and standing outside on the corner watching and waiting. He was like a well-trained dog that runs out to the edge of the yard, but never leaves it. He stood right at the very edge of the corner—almost in the street, but not quite. Once, when the bread truck man came around the corner too fast, Ben almost got clipped by the rear bumper of the big van; he was that close. But that was his spot, his place to watch the town wake up, his personal viewing angle on his familiar little world. Ben was no fool. He knew that whatever days were left in this world would go right on by—with or without him; and he figured it was best to keep an eye on each and every one of them from a good vantage point—or some of them might slip by without being experienced and unappreciated or entirely unnoticed. When your days are numbered, this just won't do.

To most people, Ben only seemed to have two things that took him away from his constant daily vigil. When the Cubs were playing, he would take out his ragged old blue and green lawn chair and sit in the sun on the sidewalk in front of the shop near the bench that no one had ever sat on; his transistor radio next to him on the concrete. He always wore his tan jacket, no matter how warm it got. Even a slight chill was hard to accept anymore at his age. When the game started, he leaned back in the chair crossing his legs and faded away to Wrigley Field. The little store across the street became the right field fence, and the old two-story hotel changed into the giant scoreboard. The manhole in the center of the intersection became the mound, and his corner became home plate—and for a time, Ben assumed umpire duties while the afternoon went somewhere.

On Wednesdays, Ben would pull the gray tarp off of the old red and white Schwinn that he kept out behind the shed, stuff a couple of garbage bags in the metal baskets on either side of the back wheel, and head out of town on the county road picking up aluminum cans for the recycling truck to pick up on Saturday morning. This was Ben's way of doing his small part to keep America beautiful. He felt a little like the old Indian in the TV commercial that looked out over the land with a tear in his eye. He was disappointed with the pollution and exploitation of the natural environment--and especially littering, and his weekly foray into the country to pick up cans was Ben's way of helping out a little. He found it hard to believe that people would actually throw empty cans into the ditch along the road—especially when they were worth a nickel each. Most people who had been through the great depression had a certain appreciation for the value of things, and Ben was no exception. Oh, it was easy to see that one can wasn't of any great value, but a garbage bag full of them were worth a dollar or three—and one could pick that many up in ten or twenty minutes sometimes. It wasn't a significant income, but it was a little extra spending money—nothing wrong with that. And besides, it meant getting away for a while—out of town, away from the corner, away from the daily routine of watching and waiting.

Can day, as Ben called it, meant getting up early--with the sun and the birds. He would wheel the bicycle around to the front of the shop and look it over to make sure the tires were up and the seat and handlebars were tight. One wouldn't want to get two miles out of town and have to fix or adjust something—not with all the tools back at the shop. Then he would go inside and grab a few garbage bags, a snack for later, and his navy blue cap with "Chicago Cubs" in white lettering--and then he would ride east out of town picking up cans along the county road for much of the day. Sometimes, he would turn north and work his way up the hollow to the top of the ridge overlooking the river valley, then turn around and coast all the way back to town; often in time for the afternoon ball game.

One Wednesday morning, shortly after the town and the sun woke up; Ben got his things together and set out on his usual route—eastward, out of town. Just beyond the village limits, the other county road turns off to the north and follows the hollow up to the ridge. He decided to go this way, stopping every hundred yards or so, and then walking along both sides of the road rescuing cans from the grassy roadside ditch. It was a nice day, but the cans came slowly. After almost three hours of diligently working his way up the hollow, Ben only had a little over a bag full of cans. But the day was still young and he felt good about being away from the corner for a while, and although it was a few miles back to town, it was all downhill and he could coast the entire distance in a few minutes. He thought he would go a little farther than normal this time—not much, maybe another mile or so.

At the top of the ridge, the county road veers to the east and stretches straight as an arrow for miles, with only a couple of dips in the road—no problem for the Schwinn. Ben usually didn't go this far, and as he pedaled, he felt invigorated by the fresh air and country smells. He followed the road eastward for a short way and after a while realized that he hadn't even stopped to look for cans. This surprised him, somewhat, but he was having a good time and he felt good. It wasn't all that late, yet, and so he continued on—just for the ride; his bag of cans tied onto the top of one of the rear baskets. He even found himself pedaling a little faster and leaning a little more forward on his seat.

This was really living; to get away and enjoy the warm sunshine and pungent smell of alfalfa and mustard weed. He wondered why he hadn't taken a ride--for the sake of riding—before this. He had the entire road to himself, mostly. Hardly a car even went by, and there's nothing like the sound and feel of a country road with no traffic. Red-winged blackbirds fluttered from fencepost to fencepost coaxing him further along. Cows looked up from their eating chores to pay respect. Hogs in the distance clanged their feeder doors to the tune of locusts and robins, while the distant sputter and clatter of tractors and hay rakes kicked up dusty clouds in the rolling fields bordering the road.

After a while, Ben took out the Snickers bar he had stashed in his jacket pocket. It was all the lunch he needed—and he didn't even have to stop to eat it. He wasn't really hungry, but it was there, and... well... He continued on at a steady pace, nibbling on the Snickers; knowing that going a little farther would be OK. Nothing else really seemed to matter, actually. He just felt like he needed to keep going. He went by farms he used to know, and the old cheese factory, now closed. Farther down the road, he knew he would come to the state highway which continues east all the way across the state. It became somewhat important, now, to make it that far—just to the state road. He knew he could do it. He leaned into the breeze and pedaled a little faster still, seemingly getting more energy as he went. He thought about his wife back in town, sitting by the window watching the afternoon talk shows on TV. She wouldn't mind that he was gone longer than usual as long as there was no trouble. They always had a little agreement that, "No news is good news." If something goes wrong, call—or else someone else will; if not, everything is fine. He wondered if anyone would even notice that he wasn't sitting in his usual spot in front of the shop window listening to the game. He didn't think anyone would mind—not even the Cubs—and Ben certainly didn't either—not today. The Schwinn flew along like it had been made especially for this occasion. It gave him a kind of power. The kind he had forgotten about a long time ago. The kind that made him feel young again—and in control.

It seemed like no time at all when Ben came to the end of the county road. The pavement made a little curve to the left and stopped perpendicular to the state highway which, to the left, went northwest down another hollow for several miles, and to the right, went straight east all the way across the state. There was something more to this intersection, though, than Ben was able to see. Signs pointed to what was this way and that, but it was also a boundary line of sorts—a place where the dog might go beyond the limits of its yard to an unplanned, unsanctioned adventure into the unknown. It was the line between what was expected, and what was considered prudent. It was an invisible line that everyone encounters at some point in his or her life; and often, it is crossed without the slightest inkling that it is there at all.

When Ben got to the stop sign, he didn't. He rounded the corner to the right without the slightest hesitation, and headed east on the paved shoulder, not even seeing the cars whizzing past. He was pedaling harder now, and the Schwinn lunged forward as if on a mission. He had plenty of room on the blacktopped shoulder of the highway; the long white line leading him ever eastward into the fading light. He no longer noticed the red-winged blackbirds or the smells of the fields going by. Now, a faint oil smell from the highway lured him ever forward. He no longer thought about his corner, or his wife watching the soaps and game shows. He didn't miss the action at Wrigley Field, or the cans that he passed by without a glance. Nothing seemed to matter at all anymore. He just kept going. He had no conscious thoughts about the irrationality of it all. He only knew he had to just keep going.

The slow transition from afternoon to evening went completely unnoticed as Ben pedaled relentlessly onward. He felt nothing as he pushed faster and faster—except perhaps, a vague and urgent sense of freedom. It was as if he were outrunning something that had long held him back. He was so intent on continuing forward, that it didn't matter to him where he was going. He simply knew he had to go there. But he was already there in a way--he had gone beyond his boundaries; beyond anybody's boundaries. He was no longer aware of his trusty Schwinn carrying him away on the paved highway. He wasn't old anymore--and the aches and pains that had followed him around these last several years disappeared from his notice. He no longer pedaled the bicycle along the road; he now glided effortlessly above it; his legs hardly moving. Everything passed by in a blur--the cars, the fields, the farms, the day—everything.

The flashing lights were like a distant call from a far off place. He wasn't even aware that they had come up behind him and were keeping pace with him. The voice on the PA speaker was small and hard to comprehend, and the order to pull over went right past him with the passing cars. It was as if the entire world had faded back somewhere behind him as he propelled the old bike onward with every bit of energy he could muster. Without even thinking, he tried desperately to outrun... something; his past, his future, his existence.

But something inside him continued to hold an unseen grip on him. Without thinking, he slowed down, first just a little, then a little more, until the old Schwinn rolled to a stop on the shoulder. The front wheel turned to the side as he stood straddling the bike looking eastward with a blank stare. He only vaguely heard the voice of his wife running up to him, crying out his name with worry and relief. It was hard for him to see through the tears that had soaked the front of his jacket. He didn't even remember the ride home at all.

The next day was one of those perfect summer mornings that everyone remembers fondly. The sun came up over the ridge big and red and on schedule. Robins announced that the day had started, while the occasional car yawned off to work. A lawnmower across town told of daily routines starting. Ben stood at the edge of his corner watching intently. His shoulders seemed to sag a little, but he watched and waited with the same diligence as always-- for he was no fool. He knew that whatever days were left in this world would go right on by--with or without him; and he figured it was best to keep an eye on each and every one of them from a good vantage point—or some of them might slip by un-experienced and unappreciated or entirely un-noticed—and this just won't do.

Popcorn Night
(3-14-95)

Tonight I'll fill the popcorn bowl
It's been a, sort of, day-long goal
And while I watch a favorite show
I'll empty it again, you know

Sometimes yellow, sometimes white
I think that I'll have both tonight
I'm probably somewhat self-abused
With too much salt and butter used

It happens every Tuesday night
A well anticipated rite
With orange juice to wash it down
And four remotes all lying 'round

...another excerpt from a book that didn't happen...

Happiness is fleeting. It usually doesn't last. There isn't a magic recipe for it, and there isn't a surefire way to find it, keep it, or sell it. The best you can do is appreciate it when it comes, enjoy it for as long as you can, and then hope it returns soon and often. I think contentment is what we really want. How do I know what we really want? Simple. We're all alike and we're all different, but I never met anyone who wanted to be discontented or unhappy. Therefore, everyone must want to be content or happy. There—that was easy, wasn't it. I can write whatever the hell I want here.

The way I see it, contentment is more of a long-term thing—kind of a general sense of feeling kind of good about things. You can even get mad and still be generally content with life—at least by my definition. The trick is to figure out what you can do to find that feeling—and then actually DO those things. We're good at thinking about things, but most of us are pitifully bad at doing the work. I always say, "Thinking is not doing." So DO something, damn it. Don't just sit there and blame others for your circumstances. Don't justify ANYTHING—including why things are the way they are. YOU have absolutely ALL the control over the part that you play in everything. Sure, there are a lot of outside forces at work all the time, but there are always two sides to everything: the side that you can do something about, and the side that you can't. That means that at least 50% of EVERY circumstance is within YOUR power to change. This is important. Just think about this—If you can get into a mindset that says, "I have the power to improve at least HALF of all my problems, or halfway improve ALL of my problems" then you really can make a substantial difference in how things are going in your life. Then—and here's the hard part—if you actually DO something to make those changes for the better, then you will see positive results—and you just might feel better for it. Happier? Yeah, happier. There's a difference between *happy* and *happier*, though. Don't shoot for happy—you'll fail. But even a small improvement in your life can make you happi<u>ER</u>. THAT small gain is easily attainable if you put a little effort into it. A whole bunch of those small gains add up to contentment. That's what I think. That's what I try to do.

Seeing
(4-8-96)

There's nothing like a blind person to make us really see
We see so little of our dreams on our own
With our long-accustomed eyes and blank stares
The way we slouch back in our favorite chairs

Someday I might see like the sightless see
And I might just know what came over me
And I'll lean forward on the edge of my seat
And take a real good look around

In Heaven
(9-8-95)

It was still very early and barely first light
And sleep was still with me, though no longer night
And in through the window from out on the lake
The lonely hello of a loon made me wake

I thought as I rose that a morning is best
When even though early, a good night of rest
Is followed by breakfast prepared on a fire
And no one who's done that would call me a liar

The boat was a cloud and the lake like a mirror
I smelled bacon and eggs as an island drew nearer
And then I was there and I saw it for real
It didn't take long to make history the meal

And then I went fishing instead of to work
And thought of co-workers back home with a smirk
But just for a moment, and then it soon passed
I'm here for the moment—in heaven at last

We don't hear certain words as much these days as we probably should. When was the last time someone described someone else to you as having integrity... or as being honorable? In our everyday conversations, we don't talk about forgiveness and redemption and spirituality and kindness. We might very likely hear that someone is cool... or really nice, but not generous, or honest, or even friendly. I, for one, would very much like to be thought of as honorable and kind instead of cool or "an ok dude". Maybe it is time for a grassroots resurgence of these more descriptive and meaningful sentiments. Maybe the cold, modern world can use some old-school, heartfelt compliments and positive, encouraging reinforcement. And maybe I should put my money where my mouth is (thinking is not doing).

Honor
(4-10-96)

In truth, we all should make our mark
If only to avoid the dark
Imagined feelings in the night
That only truth can bring to light

With due respect, when duly earned
We'll likely see our fortunes turned
And live a full and fruitful life
With fewer petty woes and strife

In caring, is our value set
A measurement of what we get
When what we reap is what we sow
A question not of who we know

And when we go our money stays
Unless one gives, one surely pays
For only honor fairly won
Will last when all is said and done

Natural Light
(3-10-00)

There in the natural light
I see as I'm seen likely
In ways, but not them all
And measured anyway—as we tend to do

Seeing is believing
In air that is clearly clear
With eyes that sometimes blink
And miss some things—as they sometimes do

And so the me I see
Is missing some of me
Or missing some of you
The way it has to be—the best that I can do

Higher Ground
(5-8-00)

In a time of rediscovery, in a revelation void
A fool would look away in consternation
There's a place in our society for a friar or a Freud
A cool refreshing breath of conversation

It's an errored indiscretion in a misbegotten pact
When fair consideration is forsaken
And "Everyone is equal" is a long-forgotten fact
When lucky people find themselves mistaken

On a wisp of inspiration, born of circumstantial fate
A tale of better times can be related
The villainous antagonist falls victim to his hate
To render better days anticipated

If ever there was an intangible, ill-defined and difficult-to-attain goal in our pitiful lives, one of the most fleeting and elusive among them would be "a better life". With even the most minimal of effort, anyone can make life "better"; but how much better should life be in order for us to proclaim it better? I tend to believe that ANY improvement, big or small, is worthy of celebration—or at least, recognition. A number of small improvements can truly build up to a substantial and valued positive change. Even one big improvement, perhaps with a few small ones, could mean a life-changing event. So if my philosophy is valid, the little chuckle we get from a goofy poem might very well be the insignificant grain of sand that makes the needle on our scales start to swing the other way. We

might want to consider paying closer attention to these
small "gains". Maybe we should all work on our powers of
appreciation a bit. Maybe that, alone, might make us a
somewhat more contented bunch. ...works for me.

Things of Gold
(9-19-02)

With never time enough for things of gold
A penitent past has grayed with old
And fraying bindings no longer tight
That let things go, for wrong or right

And though our heaping plates hold much
That tastes of pain, regret, and such
There also grows a solid root
Of flowered vine and tasty fruit

For every bitter bite of black
Another two of whiteness stack
Upon a new and growing pile
Of heartening strength and loving smile

So now the things of gold burn bright
With shadows blinded by the light
Of good and rightful days of peace
While darkness earns a cold release

Hope is a peculiar human idiosyncrasy. We all somehow know what it means to hope, but we are hopelessly lacking in using it as a guideline to improve our lives; to give us direction. All too often, we leave it to others to manifest our hopes for us. It is, sometimes, thought of as a kind of inevitable fate that our hopes come to fruition somehow. We might even put our faith in our chosen deity to provide us with the things we hope for. But while we do this, and all of us are probably guilty of it, ultimately we each have, by far, the greatest potential for realizing our hopes and dreams. With a small measure of self-awareness and a pinch of commitment, we could start ourselves on a path to realize our desires. Easier said than done? Maybe. But what have we got to lose? If we don't have something, we won't have less of it by not trying to get it.

The Big Improvement
(2-11-96)

Its odd, you know, the look of stone
Which changes by the artist's hone
And lives a new and special life
The son of chisel, hammer, knife

But then what happens—after birth
The fools will bicker over worth
And never really understand
The big improvement here at hand

That Day
(9-13-05)

There are days when hearts go somewhat slower
When sadness rises and takes us lower
Days are dark and time will creep
While nights are full of restless sleep

And anger finds its way to being
Some of what our friends are seeing
Though they know it cannot last
And soon will fade into the past

But these are days like all the others
Born of happy, hopeful mothers
Each a chance to make the best
If only we can pass the test

So these are days we must hold dearly
Each a chance to see more clearly
Hearts don't have to go that way
This doesn't have to be that day

The Present

Who will hear a new heart beat
with ears gone old and cold with pain
Who will see new lessons learned
when hopes have trickled down the drain
And who will offer all there is if there is little left to give
A fool, perhaps, or saintly soul
who still has yet more life to live

How does someone use the truth
when many truths were only lies
How can one profess to see
when born and raised with blinded eyes
And how is real redemption found
if trust is kept with lock and key
It isn't, maybe, truth be told—but maybe it sure ought to be

What are words if tossed like dust
upon the wind, forever lost
What are promises grey with age
whose value lags behind their cost
And what are thoughts but shadows
caught like nothing moving nowhere fast
The future is the present soon,
but the present never was the past

The Worker
(12-15-93)

When night time comes to end the day
Like curtains after some fine play
And worthy work is done so well
That anyone would gladly pay

I, for one, feel really good
For giving everything I could
And if I long to rest a spell
I've earned it, so I surely would

And when the morning ends the night
I hope to always start it right
And so, when all is there to tell
I hope I stand in worthy light

Sometimes, a story is just story. It doesn't have to have a lofty moral or a hidden meaning. It doesn't necessarily have to have social significance or even a particular literary worth. It doesn't even really need to be read by anyone. This is such a story—lacking in many ways and really quite uninteresting. It is, however, "based on truth" again. The names were changed so as to not embarrass the insignificant. The walk actually took place—in a real place, but the severity of the "problem" is exaggerated. Locals might actually know where this happened if they happened to be of the nature walk persuasion.

Larry's Walk
(10-9-00)

Larry had one of those teeny tiny slivers in the bottom of his left foot. You couldn't find it if you tried--it was so small, but it sure hurt. I don't know why something that small has to hurt that much. It just doesn't make sense. Anyway, it tends to put a damper on everything when you're out for a walk in the woods.

It was about—oh—quarter to six or so, and he and Bev had just finished supper. It didn't get dark until around eight, so Bev asked if they might take Abbey, their four year old lab for a walk down the hollow to the Wisconsin River bottom and back. So Larry slipped on his Adidas and they headed out behind the house--down the path toward the woods in the ravine—Abbey leading the way.

It was really nice out—one of those perfect September days—bright and clear, not too hot, not too cold. Just right for walking. They entered the woods on the path that Larry had mowed around their property. It ended just inside the edge of the woods though, since it was too steep for the old John Deere rider, and since the ground in the woods never really seemed to dry out, Larry was afraid the tractor would get down to the bottom just fine—but stay there forever. There was a hint of a beaten path the rest of the way to the creek that trickled down to the other creek that disappeared somewhere on the way to the river. They hopped over the wet bottom of the ravine and made their way up the other side to where the mowed path started up again and veered off to the left, up the ravine through the main body of the small woods, and eventually breaking into the field where it circled back toward the house. They veered right though, ducked through the barbed wire fence, crawled under another one, went up over a small ridge, crossed another smaller ravine, and went over the next ridge between two fences that allowed cattle to get from one ravine to another without using up much of the tillable land at the top of the ridge. They then continued down an old logging road that criss-crossed the creek all the way down to the state park fence. I'd say it had to be at least a mile from the house to the park fence—and maybe another half mile to the river from that point.

Now those little slivers can be pretty painful, but usually you can stand it. After a day or so it just kind of goes away. But when you are walking up and down hills, it gets an extra little nudge now and then that you wouldn't ordinarily have to experience. Larry was getting a bit uncomfortable and stopped at the park boundary fence to take his shoe off. He still couldn't find the sliver, but there was kind of a little red spot that he scraped with his fingernail to see if he could catch the end of the sliver and make it stand up enough to get a hold of. No luck, though. Abbey came up for a sniff and decided to move on. Bev offered to turn back saying that the walk wasn't that important. If he was in pain they should just go back. Larry explained that it wasn't that big of a deal and that they could go on.

He put his sock and shoe back on and stepped carefully up a log that had fallen on the fence and jumped over to the other side wincing as the sliver gave him another jab. Bev followed and after a few yards they came upon a fairly wide path that was obviously maintained. Someone had used a chainsaw to clear fallen trees off the path, and there was the look of occasional foot traffic. The creek had dried up a distance back, but the path meandered back and forth across the bed almost all the way to the river. The ravine wasn't a ravine anymore. It had become a small canyon-like valley with rock outcroppings and very steep sides that rose about four hundred feet to spectacular bluff overlooks. It was a very nice walk, and Abbey had a wonderful time trotting up one side, then the other looking for dog stuff. It was beginning to get a little dark, though. Down in the bottom of the valley the sun had set hours ago and soon it would set up top, as well.

They came to a sign where the path forked within sight of the river. One path went back up the valley wall at an angle toward the camping area on the bluff. The other followed the river bottom west along the foot of the bluffs for about three quarters of a mile to the railroad bridge that crossed the river into town. A bench sat near the sign and another smaller path—almost unnoticeable—led to the river bank about a hundred feet away or so. Bev asked if they could carry the bench over to the river's edge to sit a while, and Larry said it would be a good idea. His foot was smarting a lot and he wanted to take another look.

Abbey went right into the water and swam in circles-- looking for potential ducks to retrieve, no doubt. Bev commented on how peaceful this place was, and how they would have to come back when they had more time to enjoy it. Larry had his sock off again and noticed that he had a sizeable red welt now that was getting pretty tender. And to make matters worse, it became obvious that they would not make it back home before it got dark. Much of the way back was overgrown and without a light you could easily walk right into a branch and lose an eye or something. Larry suggested they get moving. It was going to be a challenge to get back without trouble.

They replaced the bench and backtracked up the path to the place where it turned right up a smaller ravine—they guessed it went up toward the park office which was at the south end of the park and about two miles from home. It was time to make a decision. They could continue up the main valley in the dark through brush and overhanging branches, crossing the creek several times and risking getting hurt, or they could go right—up the wide park path to the office, onto the blacktopped road and walk two more miles in a roundabout trek on the county road. There was also another complication: Abbey had never been taken for walks along the road before this. Bev wasn't sure she would know enough to stay out of the way of oncoming cars. And one other thing—Dogs in the park were supposed to be on a leash.

There wasn't time to spend pondering their choices. Larry's foot was hurting seriously now, and it was quite dark. They decided to go the long route. At least that way they could see better since the path was wide and clear, and they could stop at the park office and call someone if Larry's foot was too bad to walk on. He was already limping, and they estimated a half mile walk up the ravine to the office.

It turned out to be a little farther than that, though-- and uphill all the way. By the time they reached the top of the bluff, Larry was favoring his good foot a lot, and tried not to show the pain that was written all over his face. They walked through a tall grass field toward the park office on the path which had become a two lane dirt road. It was totally dark now with no moon to help out. The stars were quite bright, and Bev swore that there were never more in the sky as on this night. Had it not been for Larry's bad foot, it would have been one very nice walk—however long it turned out to be.

When they came to the blacktopped park road, Bev became concerned that they could get a fine for not having Abbey on a leash. Larry assured her that whoever might come along would understand that they had a predicament, did the best they could, and could not be blamed for not following the rules to a "'I'." He did, however, pull his belt out of his loops and string it through Abbey's collar making a rudimentary short leash. Abbey pulled hard and choked herself to the point of labored breathing—like dogs always do.

It was only a couple of hundred feet around the bend to the park office and both of them felt that their misadventure was nearly over. One quick phone call and someone would come to pick them up. Good thing, too, because Larry's foot was hurting badly. When they came around the edge of the trees lining the road, they could see to their dismay that there were no lights in the office. It was closed. Bev said that she thought for sure that it would be open until eleven. It wasn't. A small bench outside the entrance was just what Larry needed, though. Another check of the sore foot showed a deep scary reddening that indicated a festering infection. Somehow, though, they were going to have to walk the two miles or so along the county road outside the park--limping all the way. Abbey, at least, could run free, and they would have to try and keep her out of the path of cars going by, but it turned out that there weren't many cars. A sign at the park entrance warned of a bridge out four miles down the road. That, at least, would keep traffic to a minimum.

It was after nine when they reached the intersection of the two county roads. Larry was in great pain and limping badly. Abbey was doing OK, and keeping pretty much to the side of the road. Bev was concerned about Larry, but knew that there was only about three fourths of a mile to go. It wouldn't be long and they would be home. They turned north on their road and continued past a small herd of young cows that kept a steady vigil on Abbey--who was staying nicely to the side of the road. Larry thought about taking his shoe off and just walking on the edge of his foot, but decided to weather the pain and trudge on.

They came to the edge of their twenty one acre property and crossed down into the roadside ditch, up the other side of it, and through the fence onto the trail that came out of the woods and circled around to the house. Larry could see the house now, only a hundred and fifty yards away. It was silhouetted against the northwest sky which was lit up by the lights of the town. He was in great pain, but felt he could make it. The driveway was only a couple hundred feet more. Bev moved ahead to open the garage door while Abbey found her dummy toy and trotted around looking for someone to play with her.

At last, they were in. Bev helped Larry to get his shoes off and he limped off toward the bedroom and a shower.

Later, in robes, they sat for a while thinking about the night. Larry had his foot up on the deck rail. It was still throbbing, but the shower and the beer did wonders, and he knew—with a keen certainty—that tomorrow would be TV night.

Once in a while, my wife and I will venture out into the world on the occasion of our anniversary—or some other special time. We have found that the unique experience at each bed & breakfast makes for an interesting, and usually somewhat memorable, time. Most are run with an obvious nod to the quaint and romantic. Many are a weekend trip back to a quasi-Victorian age—or at the very least, a step out of the normal modern-day routine and into another world where the average working couple can be waited on and pampered for a day or so. The breakfasts are nothing that normal people would normally eat. But they are almost never bad and almost always worth the anticipation and the debit card transaction.

Margaret's Room
(6-26-10)

And so we find ourselves at last
In Margaret's Room where all the past
And precious things we hold so dear
Have fated us to end up here
Together as it ought to be
So many years of you and me
No one knows where life might take us
When we leave today, it might just make us
Think about important things—if we are smart
And maybe keep them in our heart

The Day After
(8-29-94)

The sun is out, the sky is clear
And even though it's morning here
The yearly night we hold so dear
Will last, again, another year

It's funny though, I have to say
How far we go so we can stay
For just one night and just one day
And then, again, we're on our way

But this is special, very nice
As if there never was a price
Including pink champagne on ice
And lots of fun, to be precise

But now it's time to go, I see
And this will be a memory
We both are leaving happily
Looking forward to what will be

We Were Here

So cold these days of falling leaves
The end of warmness one believes
A prelude for the snowy grey
Misfortune of a winter day

The years pretend we never age
But all of us will turn a page
And then another, then another
Soon enough, there is no other

But we were here and going there
We could have been most anywhere
A cozy room and friendly meal
The never ending feelings real

Another year alas is gone
The leaves will find another lawn
To grace again this coming year
Reminding someone we were here

Over the years, I have come to appreciate, more and more, the feelings of others—and although it is most apparent when something significant happens—like a death or a birth or a new car, I am making a conscious effort to be more empathetic for the more mundane events in people's lives. I have come to believe that if I can put myself in the place of someone who is having difficulty writing a check in the checkout lane, I might be able to not only understand how they feel, but also avoid a senseless reaction of impatience on my part—which does no one any good. I might even acquire a desire to actually help someone that I might otherwise have gotten upset at—and I should think that nothing but good could come from that.

Death, however, finds a more significant place in our lives as we age. No doubt, our own inevitable and certain death begins to make us think about our lives—and the lives of others, but even people who are really quite unlike each other will find they have this experience in common at some point. The requisite condolences, therefore, become more heartfelt, and the Hallmark card is no longer enough to express our sympathy. We meaningfully wish a real comfort for those who suffer a loss of a loved one. In my case, I no longer simply say, "I'm sorry. You have my condolences." I now say things like this:

The Light In The Hollow
(For Barb Tubbs)
(8-6-07)

The small woman dropped off some cookies again
For no special reason—she did now and then
She chatted a bit, about birds and the weather
And how it's so fine to be neighbors together
Like a cool welcome breeze on a hot summer day
She always had something of value to say
Of friendship, or sharing some good things to eat
Like chocolate and walnuts and Montana wheat
And down in the valley she spent all those hours
With hummingbird feeders and weeding the flowers
Her glow will be missed, though it's certain, no doubt
The light in the hollow will never go out

Birds of A Feather
(For Birdie Hampton)
(7-7-10)

So the memories are bound
by simpler times and humbler ways
That somehow never count for less or fade the days
Of one-room schools and moonlit nights,
of sledding in the deep, deep snow
The boys would often join in, though—
and Birdie always smiled so

The piano played in music class—
and the Grand Ole Opry flew
Like magic from the radio, and all there knew
That over at the Checkerboard
on some approaching Friday night
The sounds of county music
might see Birdie dancing by colored light

Mrs. Flicker never seemed to mind a visit to the big old tree
To see her brand new birds of a feather trying to be
A bit like all good siblings—noisy and free to fly someday
In all directions, come what may—
But Birdie found it best to stay

It wasn't always fun and games—with nuts to crack
And water to be carried from the springs out back
But oh the picked berries soon became sweet sauces or pie
That filled the tin lunch pails high—
and always caught sweet Birdie's eye

And now these recent years
have come to make us look back in joy
At the fastest typist around—with a marvelous boy
And a wonderful girl to remind us
how special motherhood can be
With kindness anyone can see—
and Birdie shared it all for free

The best of times, the good old days—and birds of a feather
Are what remains when everyone still gets together
Jack and Denny, Nancy and Mary, Dewey and Sis
And though Sam and Carmen are gone, too—
it's now Birdie we'll miss

…another excerpt from other writings…

One problem with grief is that we (…and I do mean
ALL of us) tend to think of ourselves as victims when
something really traumatic happens in our lives. That's
natural enough, I guess, but I think it is important to try to
remember one major lesson that I stumbled upon a few
years ago: we all CHOOSE how we think. All worries, all
grief, all sadness, anger, resentment… whatever… they're
all RE-ACTIONS to something that has happened to us. No
one forces us to react a certain way. We ALLOW ourselves
to react the way we do. We actually have control over it.
Oh I know the experts say depression is a chemical
imbalance in the brain. Great. That doesn't mean we have
to act the part. We can choose to react a different way. I
have some experience in this. I don't mean to say that it

works every time or that it is easy for anyone to do. I just mean that with practice, we all have the capability to ACT better. With some practice, we can begin to feel better. I never met anyone yet who got where they wanted to go by giving up.

So where am I going with this? I don't know... maybe... just start realizing that thinking positively isn't DOING things positively. Reading self-help books doesn't make your life better, DOING what's in them does. You can't just tell someone to "buck up, Bill" (wait... isn't that what I'm doing?), you sometimes have to help them—either by example or with compassion and extraordinary patience... or with a kick in the ass.

As always, the trouble is in the details. Every person is different. Every situation is different. Every fix is different. I DO believe that we have to work through our grief. But I think it would help if it was taught at an early age that we CAN work through it, SHOULD work through it, and WILL work through it if we persevere and pass it on to others. Just imagine what the world would be like if we all learned early on that we were all here to help each other and that although it is natural and normal to have loss in our lives, we are not alone—never will be, and we will get through it. Period.

You may say I'm a dreamer? Well, I'm not the only one. *(John Lennon)*

Patches
(12-20-94)

They had to put Patches to sleep yesterday
He lost all his teeth and could not eat his hay
They said he was sick, and I guess that he was
He just didn't look like a healthy horse does

But he was much older than most horses get
He had to be thirty one years old, I'll bet
And never a mean, unpredictable horse
Just ready and willing and friendly, of course

And all of these years are a treasure to keep
Remembered each night in a prayer before sleep
A gentle, devoted and trusted old friend
A part of the family beginning to end

Although I write an occasional story, it is actually quite rare that a story comes out of me in the form of a poem. It does happen however, and when it does, it tends to be flat out true—or at the very least, "based on a true story".

The Farmer
So there I was, those years ago—
in retrospect, a kid you know
With wisdom sadly lacking then,
so rarely there and gone again
But then one day it dawned on me
that underneath a pasture tree
A love-struck boy might find a way
to see his sweetheart some nice day
If only he could pitch a tent
without the farmer's paid consent
Then he, or I, might have a chance
to somehow foster this romance
And so a plan was put to seed,
though risky as it was indeed
A place was found, the tent went up—
and there I was, a fledgling pup
Barely hidden by the fence
that turned away my common sense
My hopes were clear, I had a goal—
I thought that if I took a stroll
That someone who my sweetheart knows
would give her notice, I suppose
And we might see each other's smile,
if only for a little while

101

And then it really did occur—
I heard a noise and it was her
She came by horse and found me there,
in disbelief that I was where
The farmer might just happen by—
enraged that I would even try
To squat my tent upon his land—
she knew he wouldn't understand
And sure enough, as I was warned,
he soon arrived incensed and scorned
He told me that I had no right
to pitch my tent and spend the night
I told him he was right, of course,
and promised in my cold remorse
That I was blinded by my quest
and soon would leave by his request
And then his hardness seemed to fade—
there really was no trouble made
He saw that I meant no one harm
and sighed a long look at his farm
And then he said he understood,
I only did what most kids would
And in his firm and farmer way
he told me maybe I could stay

The Prize
(1-15-95)

I saw a plastic bag today
While driving home along the way
And in it there was something black
That caught my eye and I turned back

I thought it was a pair of socks
Or something for the tackle box
Or maybe with a stoke of luck
A radio to fit my truck

But when I stopped to claim my prize
I couldn't quite believe my eyes
Of all the things I might have found
Lay ladies stretch pants on the ground

And big ones, too, I have to say
Too big to fit me, anyway
But also there inside the bag
I found the store name on a tag

And so I took them back to town
And gave the store what I had found
In hopes that someone needing pants
Might know I found them quite by chance

Backache
(1-17-95)

I have an ache in my lower back
No doubt, from exercise I lack
I've gotten by for many years
Neglectful of my body's fears

I've never really eaten well
I lose control at dinner's smell
And then I'll sit and vegetate
And change to fat the things I ate

Sit up straight with shoulders squared
I listened, but I never cared
And never lifted with my legs
So now I have a spine of eggs

But maybe, if it's not too late
I still could lose a little weight
To ease the pressure on my back
So it won't be so out of whack

The Cave
(5-2-95)

The darkness was darker than any I've seen
The air had no smell—it was perfectly clean
The absolute silence was something to see
But now interrupted by noises from me

Passages twisting and narrow and wide
And leading to nowhere somewhere inside
Crouching and crawling all muddy and wet
But I'd do it again, it's a pretty good bet

And now I'm addicted and yearning for more
A caver forever for whatever for
Bigger adventures just might have to wait
If somebody calls for a spelunking date

These days, there is a holiday nearly every week. No doubt, if one were to check on it, there would be a holiday every day—what with National Whatever Day and Something Or Other Week. Some holidays, though, are valid enough, or established enough, or ingrained enough in our heads that we find ourselves enjoying them for no particular good reason. Despite the decidedly un-Christian roots of Halloween, for example, we Americans (In God we trust) revel in the candy and parties and toilet paper trees. Christmas is no longer a celebration of the birth of Christ so much as a Santa and the kids thing—exploited to the max by just about everyone—including me. No harm done, I suppose. When we zoom out into space a few light years and turn around and look at the earth, we are just another small dim speck in an incredibly immense and nearly eternal cosmos. How important is what we do… really?

The Witches Night
(10-31-94)

Well here it is, the witches night
And sure enough, they're out all right
I saw one just a bit ago
But she was kind of short, you know
Though scary just the same

No self-respecting witch I know
Would ever stop to say hello
But this one did, I swear it's true
I wasn't sure what I should do
And asked her for her name

She mumbled something short and sweet
And pointed to my bowl of treats
I held it out and she reached in
And helped herself and grinned a grin
And left the way she came

Now one might think I'm not all there
But I saw witches everywhere
And what if I had one less treat
It might be me they'd want to eat
And I'd be all to blame

Christmas This Way
Yes it got noisy and crazy and big
And all of the food makes us eat like a pig
We spend like a banshee and send out the cards
And decorate every square inch of our yards

Yes we start early and drag on for weeks
And justify funding the Christmas boutiques
We cut down a nice little evergreen tree
And drag it inside for our neighbors to see

Yes we remember the real Christmas roots
And then bundle ourselves in our mittens and boots
We go off to church and we pay our respects
And try to be good like the preacher expects

Yes all of the hubbub and money and lights
And sometimes we tend to forget all the nights
We spend with our families and share with our friends
And that's what we really find good in the end

Yes it's alright to celebrate Christmas this way
We all can appreciate a nice Christmas Day
If we make it a time that we never regret
And think about giving and not what we get

A Once And Wondrous Chance
(6-15-09)

That good young face you've worn so well
As far as anyone can tell
Belies the hope and promise there
That soon enough you'll surely wear
The innocence and fun subsides
Unless you notice where it hides
And bring it out from time to time
To live life always in your prime

A once and wondrous chance has come
No matter where you're coming from
To find your place and make your mark
To throw your light into the dark
And glow there so the world can see
You being who you want to be
The world is big, the promise great
For those who proudly graduate

...and speaking of holidays...

As if we didn't have enough of them, we also have our own PERSONAL holidays; birthdays, anniversaries, graduations, bar mitzvah's—you name it. But since I am a bit of a preprogrammed conformist, I find myself getting right in there and perpetuating the nonsensical and irrelevant celebrations with the characteristic zeal of a Hallmark lobbyist. I like birthdays, in particular, and find myself extending them for as much as a week in order to feel special and have cake and pizza instead of gravel and twigs—and maybe a night on the town. I set a goal for myself to write a birthday poem for everyone, but there simply can't be one poem that applies to everyone—so I broke my goal up into months and began twelve birthday poems. I'm up to two.

One Good Day
In like spring and out like summer,
changing like the constant moon
Years go by with wild abandon
marked by one good day in June
What a fine and special wonder,
filled with promise, hope and dreams
Such a very special person slightly older now it seems

So another birthday comes and so another year goes by
They've been good to you so far
and no one has to wonder why
You might have been a problem child, a criminal or liar
But you became a blessing full of class and heart and fire

So have your day and look for more,
a holiday made just for you
There is no hidden reason why it shouldn't last for two
Or three, or five, or one whole month—
enjoy it how you may
It only starts in earnest on your special one good day

Julys

The warm and tender days gone by
Are only part of what we try
To make our memories represent
The precious time so quickly spent

A birthday here, a birthday there
Julys do build up everywhere
And soon enough our time grows short
And age becomes our last resort

But sometimes someone comes along
Who ages right instead of wrong
The years stand back and wait their turn
While others have no time to burn

And more Julys will come and go
If only for a lifetime, though
I wish, in earnest, nothing more
Than more Julys for you in store

Oh, what I have learned in recent years. If only I could relay in truths the sentiments I have come to know; the new and meaningful lessons that eluded me in younger years. With practice, these things would have guided me to embrace the many things of value we all encounter throughout our lives. With appreciation, I might have expressed how priceless and precious all people are—young and old, known and unknown. I could have savored the times—the many-varied, special times—and not simply let them pass by as casual occurrences to be observed from a distance. I greatly regret that these things were not pointed out to me during the time that I might have incorporated them into my everyday life. Apologies are only words, and hardly meaningful after most of a lifetime of unmeant aloofness and closed-mindedness and biases and ignorance. Yet I do apologize—to all of my friends and family. This is not a negative thing I do. It should be understood that I am rejoicing that I did not suffer these lacking idiosyncrasies my ENTIRE life. I could grieve my many years of lost opportunities for sharing myself with others, or I could make things better starting now, this very day. I choose the latter.

The Visit

With our due in our pockets
And time on our sides
We spent it like kids when a day finally comes

With a years-long attachment
And the comfort of friends
We went off to visit our family almost

With the real and the honest
And a wonderful meal
We vented our cares and made room for the new

With a curious wonder
And a couple of beers
We sent ourselves reeling back through the best of times

With a handful of kindness
And a yearning for more
We meant our goodbyes and gratefulness to last

Words Come Warm

With empty words, my thankless eyes
Would line up like the other lies
I hung so easy on the wall
Collected like dead butterflies

And oh, I practiced every day
To look like someone one would say
Is really quite a special man
But deep inside I turned away

And then a few odd years ago
I looked at what I really know
And added up my fruitful years
But zero was my total, though

So now the words come warm and real
And measure how I really feel
The kindnesses and unlocked doors
Have helped a long lost boy to heal

The Warmth
(3-14-98)

All the senseless, twisted reasons
All the pulls and tries of the night
Are small compared to one brief touch
The warmth so much like candlelight

Searing, heartless, wasted words
Flow easy from a hardened soul
But meaningless they melt away
When love is the recurring goal

So why the bitter, spiteful grief
Why the lesson never learned
A free and earnest smile given
Is also just as rightly earned

The Call

One counts the time towards a goal anticipated
Across the sky, a clearing bodes a happy time
A silver song is sung to seal the grand occasion
The great accomplishment deserves the golden prize

One looks to promise as a solid promise given
Diverted hope is better than no hope at all
The best laid plan is built upon a prime direction
The full reward is gained when answering the call

Younger Days
(12-11-95)

I'll never see the moon again
With eyes that never travel far
And now I just remember when
A star was simply just a star

It's sad to see my younger days
Fall ever slowly far behind
When now, with my enlightened ways
I see that I was long too blind

The moon was all it had to be
And stars were only there at night
My younger days have fathered me
But not without a stubborn fight

Love For Tears
(2-2-96)

The shadow goes, the light appears
The debted pay their owed arrears
Accrued for all too many years
With double payments, love for tears

Sadness
(1-30-96)

Sad times demand a mourning deeply felt
And as real the pain as that which caused it
True and earnest feelings let go
Not practiced, timed or meant for others
For sadness requires grief, not time
And not the softness of another's hand
And not the dawn of another day

The Brink
(11-19-99)

It can eat your heart if it gets a start
It can take your days in too many ways
And the lines turn downward on the face of contented souls
It'll slow you down, make a permanent frown
And there, without your knowing, you just slip away

It's the hate you feel when it isn't real
It's the jealous sneer and a worried fear
And the overwhelming sadness that can damage you
It'll make you think you are on the brink
And when you think you might be, then you truly are

I have been told that although my stories sort of convey a bit of Americana, they are a little lacking in detail. If this is true—and I think it probably is, then it would appear that what I try to express on paper does not fully manifest what I have in my mind. Although I am aware of this sad point of contention, I am also mindful of the Dalai Lama's sage advice about using negatives to create positives. I have, therefore, committed myself to making it one of my life's goals to develop my ability to look at my own writings in a subjective way—and then to DO something about any discrepancies. Henceforth, then, any new stories I write will hopefully be appropriately more descriptive.

Albert's Regrets

All people, at some point in their lives, realize and contemplate the certainty and eventuality of their own mortality. To boil it all down to some basic level, we could say simply that we live and we die. Neither is easy, but the former is considerably more palatable than the latter. The regret that accompanies death is an achingly tragic thing to live with, but we do live with it—and die with it. It is a balance of what could or should have been, and what has been. We don't need to accumulate many years to feel the loss that death invariably brings to us; but if we do live a long life, we usually regret losing all of the precious life we have stored away much more than what potentially might have come—but not always.

Albert was a good man. To describe him, people would use words such as integrity, honesty, kind, hard-working, and considerate. He wasn't an unusual or uncommon man; in fact, there was probably an Albert in every small town just about everywhere. He was the local handyman; the one people called when they found a leak under the sink, or when the sidewalk leading up to the back porch got frost heave and had to be replaced or repaired. Albert could do anything. No one knew where, or how, he acquired his expertise, but he was able and willing to fix or build anything, anywhere, any time, for anyone. And he always seemed to be able to squeeze people in, despite that fact that he was always busy. And unlike many of the local contractors, he didn't start a job, go on to another one, and then come back to finish later. He showed up promptly, did the work, finished what he started, and charged a reasonable price--especially for the elderly, knowing full well that they were on fixed incomes.

Albert lived alone in a big square house just west of town on the county road. The old, gray, lap-sided house was handed down to him from his dad who was a respected and well-liked, long-time member of the community before he passed away a few years ago. It sat on a sort of ledge that had been dug out of the bluff side, and overlooked the road, the railroad track, and the river bottoms that extended as far as the eye could see northwest to southeast. A large cottonwood tree shaded the curved driveway that circled around the west side of the house and up to the back door. Out front, and across the road, a small old shed housed his rusty van, his tools, and a good bit of keepsake junk. A half-buried limestone foundation next to the shed hinted at the barn that once hosted cows grazing the bottomland.

Albert didn't use much of the house. He just didn't need it, and boarded up the stairway door to the upstairs rooms. The old house wasn't insulated anyway, and there was no point heating more of the house than was needed. There were no curtains on the windows; old yellowed shades hung half up, half down--and were never adjusted. A small portable TV sat on a brass colored stand on wheels about six feet from the big overstuffed Lazy Boy in the dining room. A small table with chrome legs and a yellow Formica top sat nearby in the middle of the kitchen. A set of salt and pepper shakers sat in the middle of it next to a small plate with a half a stick of butter covered with cellophane. He was a poor housekeeper; oh not terrible, but the place could probably have been a little neater. He wasn't a slob. He did what he needed to get by, and that was all. His life was fairly uncomplicated—being self employed and unmarried.

Biggins was a fat old bug-eyed beagle that went everywhere Albert did. He looked like someone must have stepped on him once—making his eyes bulge out with a what-the-hell look. When he barked--if you could call it that, he sounded like someone's front wheel bearings were going out. He was usually seen tethered to a twenty foot length of clothesline rope looped around the front bumper of the van--not that the rope was needed; Biggins always laid under the van right next to where the rope was tied-- always. In the evenings, Albert would take Biggins for a run along the county road down past Longpond to the rock quarry and back; Albert driving slowly along while Biggins cranked his short legs as fast as he could to keep up on his twenty foot leash which was tied to the passenger-side door handle. The exercise did nothing to trim down the old boy—the effort, no doubt, offset by the steak trimmings that the proprietor of the old hotel in town kept in a big coffee can just inside the door of the big beer cooler. Every morning after coffee, Albert would reach into the cooler and pour the trimmings into a birdbath—sized shallow pan that was kept just outside the back door of the hotel kitchen, where Biggins could reach it on his rope.

Whenever Albert was seen driving around town in his van, Biggins was seen, too, standing on Albert's lap hanging half out of the driver's window; head forward, tongue dangling. Everyone said that the power steering must have gone out of the old van since Albert seemed to need his dog to help keep the thing on the road. They were inseparable.

Mrs. Benton, who lived in a little rented house across from the Methodist Church, had "a thing" for Albert—at least that's what everyone in town had been saying for years. Her husband had died years ago after sawing half of his first finger off while building a big box to put garbage cans in so they wouldn't be so unsightly out back near the alley. It was assumed that the infection spread to his heart and killed him because he went fast when the finger never healed right. Anyway, Mrs. Benton made sure that Albert had a good meal at least three times a week--Monday, Wednesday, and Friday. She could be seen around 5:30 on those days putting a picnic basket covered with a red and white tablecloth into her car and delivering it to his house just outside of town. She never stayed long, as it would seem inappropriate for a lady to visit a gentleman for more than a very modest amount of time. The next morning, Albert would stop on his way to the day's work and leave the basket on the step outside Mrs. Benton's side door. In return for the meals, Albert would perform more than the usual amount of odd jobs around the Benton house. And since it was not inappropriate for a gentleman to visit a lady for a reasonable amount of time, Albert's van could be seen parked in the alley behind the garage often-- sometimes even after dark.

It was generally thought that Albert had money. Oh, he never flaunted it—in fact, he never showed even a hint of prosperity at all. His house was run down; his van was old and rusty, and he never wore fancy clothes or spent money flagrantly. He shopped for food at the little country store in town, and everything else at the farm store--and that was it. But he did own a couple of small houses that he had built in the hollow between his place and town, and which he had rented for several years. It was also rumored that his dad had left a goodly sum to him when he died--all of which had presumably been saved or invested or whatever people do with money when they have it. At any rate, Albert was able to pay his medical bills when he got cancer, and didn't have to rely on the state.

His illness came slowly and fooled him for a while. The hospital over in the next county had built up a reputation for diagnostic errors and fumbled care, but it was the only hospital around; and when he went over to get his stomach problems looked at, they dismissed his ailment as "nerves." Albert found it hard to believe that stress had caused a problem since he didn't feel stressed, but he was no doctor--and the doctor was. But the pain and discomfort didn't go away like he was promised—in fact, it got worse.

As time went on, Albert began to lose weight, and his appetite waned—much to the chagrin of Mrs. Benton, who unfailingly insisted that he had to eat or he would wither away. He knew, however, that losing weight for no reason was not normal--and neither was the pain that persisted in his abdomen. He figured that he must have an ulcer or some kind of stomach virus. Finally, he went back to the doctor—who referred him up to the big veteran's hospital in the city where he was diagnosed with cancer. The prognosis was not good; he could maintain his current lifestyle as long as he could with medication for the pain, or he could undergo chemotherapy and radiation and surgery in an effort to extend his life—with no guarantees that any of it would be helpful or successful.

The morbid news didn't exactly register at first. He went home with the strange feeling that he was meant to have this happen to him. It was as if so many people get cancer that it was almost inevitable that he would get it, too. It seemed, alas, to come down to a matter of when, not if—and when was now. It wasn't until he informed Mrs. Benton of his cancer, that the realization that he was dying came to him. He bravely confronted her with the news-- and his decision to ride it out with medication—and she was furious, much to his surprise. He had expected the usual forlorn wailing and quiet understanding that all the people on TV showed in the "Made for TV" movies. Mrs. Benton was angry at him--angry because he didn't eat enough like she had warned him to—angry that he had given her the news too late for her to do anything about it, like make him take vitamins or meditate to the sound of ocean waves on tape. She was angry that fate had delivered him an unfair blow--and her, too, by default. She was angry that the buffoon of a President had cut cancer research funding, and that the local hospital didn't catch it sooner. She was angry at everything and everybody—even herself.

Albert, however, took it pretty well, as he did everything. He would miss his little world--or at least he felt like he would. He regretted that he hadn't married Mrs. Benton, but didn't think it would be fair to ask her now-- even though he knew she would do it in a second. He thought sure he would outlive the bug-eyed Biggins—and there was still a chance for that, he thought. His life had been lived day by day for the most part, and he didn't have a family to mourn for him—or for him to leave. His house seemed tired of people anyway and ready for a rest, and there were younger handymen jockeying for position in town. No one would go without a new water heater element or a new roof. No one would be unable to find someone to start the furnace for them in the fall. No one would find it unbearable to live without new siding on their garage. Times change. And people seem to adapt and go on, somehow. He didn't feel that he would be a great loss.

As far as the future was concerned, he had no idea what it would have brought him anyway—so how could he miss what he didn't know about? He felt strangely ready. Ready to die.

Mrs. Benton picked up the pace of her visits a bit. She now delivered meals nearly every night up to the big old house outside of town. She no longer subscribed to the time limits previously adhered to, and often stayed until well after dark. She went for walks with Biggins in the evening, who had no trouble keeping up with her. She also made it a point to check on Albert every morning— outwardly to show her caring and concern—inwardly to verify that this was not the day... yet.

Albert found that Mrs. Benton was quite capable of doing things that he had always thought her unable to do.

She not only straightened up his house, but also fixed the door on the back porch so that it latched. She stopped the drip of the kitchen faucet, and took her car over to have the oil changed—on time and on her own. Albert realized that he had been snowed, but he found a gentle humor in it. He loved Mrs. Benton. He loved Biggins. He loved his small life and the handyman routine. He loved having coffee at the hotel in the morning, and driving around with Biggins helping him steer. He even loved the regrets that he found himself with. He decided that a man's life can be measured by his regrets. If a man mourns the life that he will lose, he must have led a good life—that measures up on the good side of the scale. If he aches for a future that promises to be bright, he must have had an investment in it—and the loss of that potential measures up on the good side, too. And although everyone will have some regrets about things they shouldn't have done, or could have done, it is a rare person that ends up with more bad than good on his or her scale of measure. Albert thought that he measured up fairly well.

When he died, every person in town attended the funeral. It wasn't a big town, but it was a big funeral. Several hundred people crowded into the small Methodist Church where Albert had built a new kitchen into the basement. Everyone knew and liked Albert. Everyone respected him, and considered him a friend. At the cemetery, where Albert had installed the new wrought iron gate, even more people came from all around the county to pay their respects. The legion played *Taps*, and fired a twenty-one-gun salute. Then they folded an American flag and solemnly presented it to Mrs. Benton—the closest thing to family he had, and who was unanimously chosen as the appropriate recipient.

When the services were over, Mrs. Benton drove slowly into town with Biggins standing on her lap hanging half out the driver's window, head forward, tongue dangling. Everyone said after that, that the power steering must have gone out of her car since she seemed to need her dog to help keep the thing on the road.

Though I have called many places home these many years, all of my better homes were in small towns. The city was ok, but looking back, I find that it was far too noisy and unpredictable and unfriendly. Invariably, all of the small towns that I resided in over the years seemed to have a singular charm and friendly demeanor that loads easily into my bag of memories. The people were real and caring enough. The streets were safe any time of the day or night.

As far as I'm concerned, lucky people live in the country. That would make me lucky. I can get away with saying things like that because I have lived in the city, and although I truly liked it when I did, I came to realize how mistaken I had been—once I got used to living in the country. I realize that people of reasonable persuasion talents might easily list a myriad of reasons why an urban setting is a good thing, but I suspect that few who have lived in both kinds of environments would choose the city over the country. Consider my poetic, and admittedly biased, memories of the city:

The City

With heaps of garbage, alleys dark and despairing
Sirens filling the sky and no one caring
Homeless people not going home
And we, with heartburn, driving on the phone
With no wave for the passersby
And no smile for their dogs to spy
And always our locked doors and precious keys
The names of very few to please
How cold to keep our hands unheld
With only pictured flowers smelled

Then, after several years in the city, I found myself back in a small town—which I hated at first, then grew to accept as, "not really that bad", then "kind of nice", then "I'd never go back". And after a time, and long overdue, I eventually moved to the country home I now reside in— never to go back (to a town or city). With a few acres to look at for a few years, it finally dawned on my wife that the land isn't what it was meant to be. Before the settlers moved in with their good intentions and ignorance, the land was wild and free—with a proper and natural balance of plants and animals and insects and birds.

The Field

It's nice, you know... the grassy field—
a remnant of its former yield
Of clover hay and oats and corn
that soon grew full of weeds and thorn
Too bad its former master died—
with due respect he surely tried
With honest work and goodly heart
to feed us all and do his part
To make the world a better place—
a credit to the human race

But then another steward came
and self-appointed just the same
Decided that the land fared best
before man came to the Midwest
With thoughtful care and good advice,
the field was poisoned once or twice

127

To kill the tough invasive weeds
and make it ready for the seeds
That one-by-one would sink their roots
beneath the workers hopeful boots

And finally in about a year,
a compass plant would soon appear
With bergamot and asters there
like pals who gather for a fair
So slowly, like a sleeping child,
the prairie wakes that once grew wild
With goldenrod and blazing star
that grows no matter where you are
In this field of hope and dreams—
as crazy as it sometimes seems

And who would think a lone bur oak
would risk attention like a joke
And sprout itself among the forbs—
a guest the prairie soon absorbs
A fire burns from end to end
to help well-meaning workers tend
This hard-worked field to former health—
its flowers now it's precious wealth
For all to see who know the worth
a prairie has on this old earth

The Old Oak Tree
(6-5-96)

It's a tall and twisted old oak tree
That's more than twice as old as me
It's somehow proud and fatherly
With sons nearby for all to see

It's an out to pasture patriarch
With thinning leaves and knarley bark
Still strong and silent, tall and dark
That somehow missed the woodstove's spark

The mind wanders with the mundane and repeating daily tasks and routines. It, sort of, goes away for a while of its own will and for extended times. It is when it doesn't come back that we run into trouble—which is a characteristic of aging. But when it DOES come back, we are often surprised at the blank spot in our day, or the alarming lack of attention we just experienced. Sometimes, though, we find ourselves WANTING the escape; the pure joy of just letting go of everything to drift for a time in the realm of whatever. We can call it daydreaming or meditation or tuna salad, but ultimately it doesn't matter what it is called—or what anyone else thinks about it. It is a time of our own. And if, by some trick of mindfulness, we can harness the experience and appreciate it as an essential part of our existence, well... that's where poems come from.

A Week From Today

A week from today was a long time ago
When I looked out the window at last winter's snow
It didn't take long for the memories to fade
Of the breakfasts and lunches and suppers we made
In the middle of heaven, the edge of the world
The smell of the breezes and water that swirled
Around holes in the lake that our paddles had cut
On the way to a day that was made for a butt
To just sit there in peace in a trusty canoe
With fishing the only thing we had to do

And now, here it is just a week from today
The memories have come out of hiding to say
That it's time to start hearing the birds at first light
And sleep to the sound of the stars every night
It's time to make lists and go shopping for things
That only an idiot packs up and brings
On a trip where you carry the world on your back
With too little room for the extras we pack
But all of it heals and relaxes the soul
And makes us feel happy and lucky and whole

Autumn Days

With Mother Nature as our friend
Who would have thought the day would end
With angry fire in a line
Along the western borderline
Where harvest fields meet distant sky
And daytime always goes to die

But there it was as plain as day
The color screamed as if to say
"Look what I can do, you fools!"
As if to break the evening's rules
But all the while, down deep inside
We like our sunsets golden fried

And so the afternoon has passed
The autumn days can go so fast
But when they go, they go in style
Its worth a little twilight smile
The fire, though, will have its price
For soon our days will end in ice

TOM BENNETT

Being Kissed

Years went by—and far too many
More than I really care to admit
And me swept up in the normal things
That seem so normal but just don't fit

To be born blind and live that way
Accustomed to the lack of sight
There's nothing missing, nothing wrong
As normal as the day and night

But there is a problem, sure as Hell
We all were meant to really see
And when we don't—however normal
It's not like it's supposed to be

And what if I could see just fine
And went through life completely whole
And then one day a ton of bricks
Convinced me that I had a soul

I never knew why no thing mattered
I never really cared that much
I never felt completely happy
Never knew the worth of touch

And then to find a depth and value
Something vaguely, blindly missed
And needed like a good night's sleep
Like finally really being kissed

Oh, years went by, and there are many
But I can use a few more still
To make up for the things I missed
And you can bet your life I will

Oh, how mundane the days can be in our lives— when we have things we do because they have always been done. We are expected to go somewhere, so we go. We make time for things not worthy of our time. But there must be something to it, alas, that we all can own up to. A bit of routine—and a pinch of the mundane—can sometimes be reassuring in a swirling confusion of ever-changing, unpredictable, perplexing days.

A toss of the head with a joking, "Ha!" An indignant waving away of the possibility. Perhaps an intrigued, "Maybe," or an exuberant, "Yes!" One gets all of these responses, and more, when confronted with the approaching date of the inevitable class reunion. Some will consider it. Some will not. Some will just have to give it a try—if for no other reason, to see how much *everyone else* has changed.

Official Classless Poem
(4-20-00)

Ok, here's a little rhyme
To celebrate reunion time
And I'll try to keep it short and sweet
So we can talk and drink and eat

So now we're all about forty eight
Bald, wrinkled, and overweight
Our ears got big with hair inside them
Our eyes got bad so glasses hide them
Aches and pains are commonplace
And brandished on our aging face
Short-term memory? Sorry to say
It likely won't come back some day

And yet we somehow all come back
To laugh at all the youth we lack
It doesn't matter if we're older
No one needs a crying shoulder
There is one thing that bugs us, though
And all of us most surely know
The years are slowly passing by
And pretty soon we'll have to... try
To take better care of ourselves so we can do this again

The Class Of 1970
(9-19-95)

So all of a sudden it's twenty five years
And all of us seem to have aged, it appears
Baldies and bellies and hair in our ears
Most of us wearing our pizza and beers

And whatever happened to all of our dreams
Some of them died with John Lennon, it seems
It's just too expensive to live by extremes
So now moderation is bursting our seams

But everything isn't as bad as all that
We'll all get together and have a good chat
And eat 'til our fingernails even get fat
And look at each other while thinking, "Who's that?"

So maybe reunions are really alright
A chance to remember old times for one night
Keeping alive the 'ol red, black and white
Friends 'till the end, with no end in sight

The night. How much has been expressed about this phenomenon of nature—full of mystery and mood, the frightful and the moonlit magic of romance? It isn't difficult to imagine how even a small amount of inspiration might manifest itself into an occasional poem—so many of us fancy ourselves as creative types. With the darkness comes the light. With the night comes… ideas.

Going Home
(11-2-94)

It's very dark this new moon night
Without a single star in sight
The clouds have exercised their right
To mask the sky in anthracite

But in the distance I can see
A little glimmer meant for me
A lantern at the livery
Or candle in the rectory

And soon my little guiding star
Will greet me, having travelled far
A kiss, some talk, a little tea
And off to bed, my night and me

Love At First Sight
(2-14-95)

I do so believe in a love at first sight
It happened to me that very first night
I clearly remember the moment it came
And nothing, thereafter, has quite been the same

A strange and mysterious feeling arose
A certainty went from my head to my toes
Now and forever, I knew it was real
The way I felt then is the way I still feel

But few understand it, and neither do I
I really don't know where it came from or why
All I can say is I know that it's right
I'll always believe in a love at first sight

The Light

The morning waits—the sunrise finds
Its way behind the lingering night
Though purple-gold and nearly here
The darkness holds at bay the light

But soon, without the slightest hint
The glittering black will then give way
To anxious blues and baby pinks
Announcing yet another day

137

...and like the night, the tricky spells of the weather can weave magic into an otherwise plain and uneventful day. Moods change readily with the cold grey approach of a storm—or the sunny disposition of a bluebird day. Emotions rise and soar with the wind and our imaginations fall damp with the rain. The silver frost, like a diamond treasure, glitters and calls to us—and we answer with our best words.

The Rain
(11-8-94)

A heavy rain has come tonight
To visit me with all its might
And though I know it cannot last
It's pouring thick and cold and fast

And I can really feel it now
It's gotten through my coat somehow
I'll surely catch my death out here
Unless I find a fire near

But even though I'm soaking wet
It hasn't damped my spirit yet
I only have to close my eyes
To see how fast my raincoat dries

And soon I'll lean back by the stove
In blankets that my grandma wove
And listen while I count some sheep
The rain will put me fast asleep

The Mist
(12-14-95)

It isn't raining, not exactly
It's really more of a subtle mist
That hangs there hardly even falling
A trick from some illusionist

It freezes when it touches down
And then a glossy sheen appears
On every branch and twig and blade
I haven't seen the like in years

And even though the sky is gone
Behind a curtain, thick and grey
I know it will be back tomorrow
As it was just yesterday

So now I'm taking baby steps
So careful not to slip and fall
But even though the ice has come
I really just don't mind at all

Steamy Days
(8-13-95)

The green is simply not as green
As that which earlier I had seen
Darker now on leaf and bean
With summer in its hot routine

The morning sun of gold and red
Is now an angry white instead
Hanging slowly overhead
To fill these steamy days with dread

Clouds that once were puffy white
Are off today and out of sight
The sky once clear and blue and bright
Is thick and hazy noon 'till night

And so I watch the weather map
For lightning, rain and thunderclap
To finally bring a colder snap
Restoring normal hues perhaps

I realize full well how quaint and tedious my cutesy rhymes can be. I would doubtless be the fighting first in line to make my escape from a room full of my own works. The incessant positivity. The cruel and polished honesty. The oversweet lack of bitterness and reality. But it doesn't have to be that way. The cover poem explicitly says, "...only words of truth and good are good enough." But maybe it might be alright to get a little real sometimes. Even the negatives inherent in reality can be seen as reasons to make something better in our lives. Even the low feelings that come with adversity or absurdities can be the catalyst for positive change—which makes the negatives positives, after all.

Hmmm

Oh, I know, I know...I've seen the stars
go swirling endlessly in their perfect arc
And I get it... the republicans reek
of hidden power agendas and money friends
It's quite obvious... our excesses and indiscretions
will haunt our holy ghosts
And yes... our excellent water
will give us whiter whites and bankable dividends

Oh, I see it… the grey brown foam
collecting behind the log jams
And it's very plain… how blood
gets increasingly easier to see
Tell me again… that my dollar
can make a difference if I act now
And yes… I will surely confess my sins
to someone made like me

Oh, I hear it… the sound of technological
progress and perpetual motion
And the glare, the glare…
of all the cars and TVs and city lights
It's amazing… that I, too,
may have already won a million dollars
And yes… every crime is a violation of civil rights

Oh, I know, I know… I'm not telling you
anything you didn't already know
And I get it… the democrats
are a bunch of commie, pinko, fags
It's quite obvious… global warming will… will…
Hmmm… I think I'm getting a hangnail

Is There
(1-30-96)

Is there nothing we have done
that overshadows what we haven't
Is there something we didn't do
that could have been what we did
Is it really ignorance, or stubbornness,
or an actual lack of love
Is there some importance in being right or never wrong
Is it basic human nature to neglect our self control
Is there always someone guilty or the best at passing blame
Is there ever beneficial anger or are we blind with words
Is it ever good to be so bad or bad to be so good
Is there ever a ready understanding
for us who are starved for it

The Cough
(12-5-95)

Bronchitis is what the doctor said
No wonder I am stuck in bed
With hardly strength to lift my head
And surely very nearly dead

My chest is just a hollow shell
A coughing chamber straight from Hell
With Vap-O-Rub outside to smell
And fever inside, I can tell

And every joint and muscle aches
My hair is sore, for goodness sakes
The doctor gave me what it takes
To see my fever finally breaks

Tomorrow, if I have my say
The Vap-O-Rub is gone to stay
And soon the cough will go away
The doctor bill, though, left to pay

Tuesday Night
(9-17-96)

There's a short, thick rope inside me
Tied to the base of my skull at one end
And to something in my groin at the other
Somehow, my accounting professor has twisted it
Little by little over the last two hours
Like a turnbuckle—very tight, very hard
It pulls my head and shoulders down
So I'm all hunched over, and I ache
I'm going to have to get something cold in me
To make the rope contract and loosen up
Some chocolate ice cream might do the job
And then I'll put in a Star Trek tape
And after a while, I'll untie the rope
And put it away until next Tuesday night

The Places
(10-10-99)

The place in back of the tenement sat beside the alley
Nearby lived the black man with a popcorn bag
Campbell's Soup on the three-step stoop
when they brought my brother home
And the ice cream man wouldn't park his van
for the tears of a four year old

The place in the back of the theater sat below the North
Star
Movies on the fence at night without the sound
The flaming red of the teacher's head
when I took my rug to school
And a naked run through the snow
was fun for an instigator's fool

The place out back by the railroad track
was an old two story
Underneath the bed, the village drunk was found
Waking screams from nightmare dreams—
a recurring wonder why
And a big galloot with a combat boot
kicked me right between the eyes

...then another place, and another... and at least three more
And the place set back from the road
is smack in a field of flowers
Our only neighbor now is the open sky
Pheasants, deer, a fine woods near, and a spirit free to roam
And my own two hands built the place I finally call home

Though winter yet, as I put down *these words*, Spring is not far off. March tends to be a mirror image of December in my eyes—so, whereas December often starts out mild (like a lamb) and turns into REAL winter at its end (like a lion), March comes in like a lion and goes out like a lamb—or at least it is supposed to. I really don't mind winter at all—quite the contrary, I like it. It looks nice. The ice fishing is quite poor in the summer. And who will support my local gas company if not me? But that said, it is still kind of nice to smell that freshness in the air that signals the nearby seasonal change. I saw a "V" of geese navigating northward yesterday. Know why one side of the "V" is usually longer than the other? More geese on that side.

Anyway—for me, Spring arrives when the robins come back—even though there is usually still a little snow on the ground. It is the first sign. It means the "bad stuff" is pretty much finished, and the good stuff has started. Shortly thereafter, the red-wing blackbirds will simply appear (you never see them flying back from wherever they go). There will be a short time in March before the rains come in earnest when the prairie gets burned off so that the invasive species get discouraged and the native species get encouraged. A car wash becomes a laugh. I start to wonder if I need a tank refill for the grill. It is time for the Messier Marathon.

Spring
(3-29-95)

There's green along the road at last
The woeful winter finally past
And though the air is chilly still
It isn't such a bitter pill
For Spring has come to fill the bill

It's good to see the blackbirds back
For soon I'll need my mushroom sack
And fried morels with broiled trout
Mean I will have to venture out
And cast for one or two no doubt

So I can put my boots away
And find my coat a place to stay
I'll get the lawnchairs down for good
And cover up the cords of wood
And do a tuneup underhood

It's funny every early Spring
I feel like doing everything
The sun returns to warm us all
And I'm renewed, as well, till fall
For Spring has come, at last, to call

Spring Morning
(4-6-96)

A high, clear morning creeps over the sky
Relieving the evening, a hearty goodbye
It hardly gets noticed, like nothing at all
While one curtain rises, another will fall

Nightcrawlers squirt from the mushy new ground
Like breakfast for robins whenever they're found
New flower sentinels sleepy with dew
Present their new colors as they always do

Lights are forsaken, turned off one-by-one
In deference to a reliable sun
The big glowing sunrise awash in the east
Is a promise well kept for the bud and the beast

All of us have had friends or family members who have gotten sick or injured or even died. Maladies and mortality, among other things, define us as human beings. And although we all want to be human beings, we don't particularly want to experience these very natural and normal facets of our existence. It is understandable, then, that we not only avoid and grieve these inevitable happenstances, but we also give our condolences when they happen to others. How well we can convey these feelings also defines us.

Days Come Grey

Sometimes days come grey and cold
without the noise of happy birds
A fistful, then, of tasty seeds
and trees soon fill with chatter heard

And oh, how slow the muscles move
when years of mornings are piled high
But one brief sniff of bacon cooked
can make them quick for one more try

The mailman doesn't bring much news,
the phone forgets to sometimes ring
The heart is full of loved ones, though,
who don't let go of apron strings

The eyes don't work like once they did,
and oh, we love so much to see
But even closed, the eyes still work
and see a wealth of blessings free

Our hearts go sometimes hard
or low when upkeep isn't kept on time
But all hearts mend with care and love,
a fix that doesn't cost a dime

And every person in this world
who has such weighty loads to bear
With faith, will know without a doubt
that all their friends and family care

All of us, undoubtedly, have a favorite place. Oh, I don't mean home. All too often, home really is where our hearts are, but I'm talking about a different place that isn't home. Perhaps a vacation spot or a secret rendezvous or a tree-house or even a nice shady tree in the local park. For me, the place that "speaks to me" is the Boundary Waters Canoe Area Wilderness in northern Minnesota. Maybe it was the old Hamms beer commercials of my youth or some inherent calling of nature. Whatever it is, I am drawn to the place—and have been for many years. Something about it has become an undeniable part of me that I can no more do without than food or rest or popcorn.

How Long Have You Been Coming Up Here

How long have you been coming up here boys
But how many of us can name that bird
And what's with all the late-night noise
That loon you love is barely heard

How long have you been coming up here guys
But it still takes two to carry the boats
An extra tent and more supplies
Than anyone needs despite the votes

How long have you been coming up here dudes
It isn't supposed to be euchre time
And packing in those heavy foods
To a purist—it's a major crime

How long have you been coming up here men
With a nine-pound mattress and electric pump
A sane person wouldn't do it again
'Cause hearts should always be the trump

How long have you been coming up here boys
That booze affects your sense of smell
That guy across the lake enjoys
Fresh air and trees and doesn't want to yell

How long have you been coming up here guys
The fish aren't there because of us
We didn't make those bluebird skies
And all that solidtude's plus

How long have you been coming up here men
How many mornings did you wake up sick
How many stars did you sleep under then
And how many of those memories stick

The Trip

In haste we sleep away the days
That lead to hidden windswept bays
And winding trails in fresh clean woods
With nothing but our carried goods

The special sparrow calls his tune
To make us come and visit soon
The invitation plainly states
That all who answer mark the dates

So mark the dates we surely will
The yearly week will fill the bill
A trip to make us yearn for more
Of crystal water and wooded shore

Its time to pack up all the things
We bought for what the new trip brings
Lead-head jigs and new white tails
A leech and bobber never fails

And euchre games will fill the night
While losers nurse a drink outside
But no one really loses there
The trip... is what the winners share

Although somewhat less than positive, my few odd years on this haphazard world might be seen in a positive way if flowered up with poetic narrative and followed by an eventual enlightenment of sorts. No matter how cruelly a story might unfold, with a happy ending it becomes a comedy. And everyone likes a good comedy.

...another excerpt from my unfinished autobiography...

These days of being different come like timid blades of grass in March—a gradual and imperceptible greening that becomes a uniform blanket of new color. These nights of constant memories set like stars of countless number in the west—one by one until they are all gone at evening's end. The long and twisted path of days weaves it's way from fragments of nothing, through a jumble of who's and where's, to a fateful point of new birth—and then on as being different from the rest. This blue story is blurry and slippery to the grip—fraught with vague memories and hard lessons and a mirror full of revelation and the hope of redemption.

There is no apparent cause for concern about the early days of this poor and normal boy who fairly fit the mold laid out for him. I recall bright sunshine days with ants on the sidewalk; a poor black man with the same name who offered his only gifts to me; and the sad, grey shack behind the tenement in the alley where we lived. Fragments of fleeting moments in time whirl up from somewhere to be looked at with uncertain eyes looking for beginnings. I was at or near four years old when the first of many storms blew in a flurry of change. And change, though common enough, has become the title of my story.

So now, as I struggle with the slippery past, there is a need for understanding and purpose. I have discovered a soul between the countless pebbles on the path. I have found finding as lucrative and rewarding as losing is hard and dark to the touch. I see that there is a somewhere—and that even nowhere was a place on the path. If there is one mountain that I find difficult to climb, it is the high peak of redemption. Its path has a name: understanding—and on the other side is a place called trust. I hope to get there some day.

Since memories walk by like vague, half there telephone poles going by in the fog, it is absolutely necessary to understand that time doesn't care about the order of things in my life. My poor wife will try with a fair heart to line them all up for some future display—or with the hope that order will somehow explain the past, but time makes a relentless effort to make soup of it all—with a flavor made up of the sum of its parts, but unique just the same. And no one can know just how much salt is in it—or when it was put in, or by whom.

I am convinced that my natural life was interrupted by a dark day at the age of five. The memory is lost, or hidden behind some thick curtain of my making—to protect my tender soul, which to this day languishes in a yearning search for the boy I lost that day. Although I see no black ghost, I know he is there—haunting me with a warning to pursue it no further. But I do pursue it—and I will pursue it, until the ghost becomes a man with a sheet over him—and the boy again begins to grow. Understanding comes like a late supper when you've missed lunch—when you don't understand. But I will have my supper, however late it comes—and it will taste good after such a long time in the fog.

Of all the precious things I lost that day, like an oppressive tax on the peasants, I gave up a portion of my soul that I could not afford. My sweet youthful memories were cut up into scattered pieces that would not puzzle together. My blooming trust was trimmed, and the trimmings became fear and yearning and a tinted window that I looked through to see the world. Love that should go both ways went nowhere and came from nowhere. I wrapped my innocent self in brooding anger and wound up a ratcheting key so that someday I would see the weasel. My smile became a mask that I wore for others, but that did not appear in the mirror. And worst of all, I was relegated to pay a significant portion of all my feelings to the ghost of the past as compensation for my silence. But like a corporate CEO who does not see the waste in his own company, I was unaware of my payments or debts. I was pragmatic and wise and going with the flow—while picking away at the employee pension fund. For forty five years, I built up a corporate façade with a weak foundation and no safety net. I have come to believe that my forty five years of blindness and confusion was the legacy left to me from the black ghost of that one dark day. All of what follows is a twisted tree born of black roots—a fruit tree that bears little fruit and suffers from worms and too little sun.

A sweet heart is prepared with the finest ingredients— a mother's care, a father's guidance, a pinch of pain and a pound of love. In the proper measure, a main course needs no dessert. Ignorance, however, will ruin any dish—and it is precisely this bitter sweetener that found its way into my story.

There is no bright fault to my family's dimly lit beginnings. The causes are lost in the mire of generations; the grey curtain of ignorance has only a very few hard-to-find openings through which one can get to the light. It is my cool truth that no one relative of mine has found an opening—or even looked for one. After all, would someone born blind know the poor lacking of sight? It has been my unfortunate bane that all those righteous people who shared their skewed ways with me took pains to defend their ways to the death. How could I suspect, even for a moment, that they might be wrong when I had nothing to compare to? In truth, I did not suspect—at least for many fractured and faithless years.

There are nearly no clearly defined people or events in this multicolored world of lives and times. I cannot say that I am all good or bad, or that any one person is all anything. Every retched soul is both graced and grievous—the measure of each being different for each. The attempt of one to aspire to the good of another, therefore, is an exercise in futility—based on the misconception that any foot will fit into any shoe. A truly good fit, however, is necessarily custom-made.

My first weak link was forged by the smithy of poverty. My meek father was a teenage victim of polio who found no inspiration in a life of meaningless jobs and pitiful pay. My mother was a frustrated and caring woman of potential who never found a path to gratified worth—born as she was to a family of ignorance and the learned restraint of Pavlov's dog. My dad found a place for his left leg brace in the adjustable seat of a sad yellow taxi—where the money found a friend in alcohol and the mind found a dead end street. My mother, having finished with one miserable man and his gift of two older siblings, took up with another who graced her with me. And as my early memories found a place to stay, I saw my younger brother make his first visit on a sunny spring day. So there were six of us then, in the shack in the alley—when a seemingly sudden intolerance crept onto my mother's plate and ruined her meal. My young eyes saw nothing save the move to the north where ruined relatives waited to ruin me.

So went my fatherly guidance. So went the wholeness a home would have. And so went the flowering buds of a new sapling—transplanted to the hard ground of cold unattended fields. Even the poor salary of a taxi driver soon turned missed, and the new entitlement of welfare came too little too late. My older brother was wrenched away in haste to a willing family host with no regard to the unity and sanctity of family—as a cost-saving measure. He became a guest in my life, who was gifted back by occasional visits. So went more wholeness.

Like leaves that drop one-by-one in the fall, I was next to be shuttled away in the interests of fiscal responsibility. I was home, and then I wasn't. There was no notice or fair choice. There was no choosing of where my vacation would take me. I was suddenly the barely tolerated young farmhand of my misnamed great aunt and uncle. I learned not to speak unless spoken to, and to sit silently on the floor by the table to watch their channels until bedtime rescued me for a few hours. Even the most accommodating eater doesn't like something. For me, it was onions above all else that spelled terror to my gut. I tried to obey, but I could not eat the things and went many-a-night to bed with a pocket full—which, thankfully, did not grow beneath my window.

Around this tender time, my memory shifts to the place of the black ghost. I was transplanted suddenly to another great aunt's house where four great uncles lived and shared the cost of living. Although it was a place of homemade bread smells and childhood adventures, my nagging suspicion points to one of the uncles as the fully cloaked reason I am me. I may never know what I truly dread to know, but there is definitely something dark in one of the four corners of that house.

It is odd that my mind keeps no memory of my many and sudden moves. As I said, I was there, and then I wasn't. My mother had moved a few miles to a small Rockwell town where a high school acquaintance practiced the epitome of ignorance and squalor. Having finished with two miserable men, she took up with another--who promptly found an alcoholic meanness and neglect a proper fit.

The big and old white square house anchored the corner of town and was home for a while. An aging narrow gauge railroad passed closely by on the east side and a chugging old locomotive with one rusting car made a weekly trek to a small nearby town and back in one day. The rest of the week it became a thoroughfare for rabbits. It was in this house that holidays made themselves apparent—a mental photograph of a drawer full of Halloween candy persists. My older sister, who comes out of the fog only very occasionally, was the happy recipient of an Elsie doll one snowy Christmas. I was in first grade and got a farm set. It was here that I acquired the first of my many "best friends." It was here that I began to see the troubled subplots and fractured images in my story. It was also here that my mother learned to spend so many of her nights at the bar—practicing the finer points of welfare economics.

My older brother was still farmed out and becoming a cousin—a visitor relative who no longer belonged with us. My mother became proficient at welfare, and my older sister and younger brother were foggy family members who have become vague shadows in the past. My mother's third man was a tavern master who found it easy to drink and squander what money he managed to earn working at the nearby canning factory as a brooding laborer. Alcohol makes a good dog bite, though, and meanness came to call frequently. Neglect, too, was only too frequent a visitor coincidentally coming when the bars were open. One summer night around midnight, a sound of ghosts thumping around upstairs frightened my sister, my younger brother and me. We were convinced that there was more than our imaginations up there—and promptly ran the 4-1/2 blocks to the tavern to express our fears. My mother was more than a little preoccupied with her brown bottle and her man used his ever-present disposition to send us home unsure of which of our fears might be worse. At home the noises persisted, and groaning too. Our second fearful visit to the bar resulted in the grudging return home of my mother and her man—to dispel our wild imaginings. A wild flurry of noise and confusion ensued as the local town drunk was pulled kicking and screaming out from under my mom's bed where he had somehow gotten lost and passed out. My mom was indignant. Her man was furious, and we kids were terrified. There was no sleep that night.

I was there, and then I wasn't. My great aunt and her husband—and his three brothers, had moved to a more modern home about a mile from the old place. It had electricity and white paint and space for my older brother and I to imagine ourselves pirates or explorers. A badger lived within rifle shot of the front porch, and the occasional passing car threw gravel dust billowing into the air to settle on everything like a thin coating of light tan flour. The big red barn was a vacation resort for pigeons and rats. An old windmill had been wired with an electric motor to pump water up from a shallow well. The outhouse was a two-holer, although I never once experienced a shared moment there.

My aunt was good to me, although I was still expected to eat onions—and if I didn't, the last one at the table was expected to do the dishes. I soon found dishwashing as distasteful as the reason I did them. Her husband was a good man who worked hard and was not above an occasional dish of buttered pecan. He too, though, made a weekly trek to town for an evening of poker at Alley Oops. I never saw him drunk, though, although his brothers were all adept at it. Although I simply cannot recall my black episode(s), I am certain that one of the brothers is my haunting dark spirit that took a piece of me to his eventual grave. As in all lives, there are times of joy and sorrow. Mine was no different, and my protective curtain partitioned off the dark corners so that I could live in a sort of adjusted consolation comfort. But I was young and did not know that I was only delaying the inevitable tightly wrung knots that would twist up inside me for decades. It would take a considerable toll and demand a stiff price to unravel. And it would take patience and time for understanding and trust between my wife and me in later years. Truthfully, as of this telling, my true colors are true only to me, and my fairly recent parting of the curtain allows no one a well-lit glimpse of my stage set—save me.

During this forced visit to my great aunt's, my older brother and I rekindled a family connection of sorts. It became the basis for a confrontation later that brought out the anger in me and the hate and resentment of other family members. It was good, though, while it lasted.

The three great uncles faded away one-by-one into the fog that I whipped up around my sore and sagging shoulders. One played the violin—not a fiddle, but the violin. He is the only family member who I can assign my musical leanings toward. One was a wanderer, who came and went from my Aunt's house for weeks at a time and who saw the world through the bottom of a beer bottle. One is a mystery to me. He was simply there most of the time---and is the primary suspect in my quest for a dark truth, although I cannot say why.

A young soul is too easily pricked by the countless pins and needles in a life of thistles. My older brother became my great aunt's only son while I was seen to have a false claim to him. While he found trouble wherever it hid, it was me who paid for it with looks of disgust and snide comments. It wasn't long before a mixed jumble of feelings made a confusing mess of my sensibilities. I wanted to go home.

And all of a sudden I was home—back in the second grade in the small town where my mother had left my sister, my younger brother and me in charge of the big white house while she wrestled with her allegiances. I had no idea how I returned or why or for how long it might be. Alcohol and ignorance and the twisted rope of a wasted life combined to make a shambles of my mom's relationship with her third man. Before the year filled out, we moved to another small town several miles to the north—away from the man whose name now meant abuse and fear. But as it turned out—it wasn't far enough away.

This new town had new friends, and a new house which wasn't new, and a new school. There were new adventures born of a child's resiliency. I learned to explore—and steal—and lie. I learned to fend for myself from morning until well after dark out of a need to separate myself from the house of poverty and stress and the third man who had found us not quite far enough away to break ties. This new town had even more bars and I learned to keep the stale smell of cheap beer in a handy place where I can smell it to this day. I had my first recurring nightmare here where in a poor kid's mind a giant could reach his big arm in through the upstairs bedroom window just touching me—but not quite able to get a grip. I cried frightened to my mom who screamed for me to go back to sleep from the couch below the register in the bedroom floor—while the third man punched her in a drunken rage and the house got very cold.

I was there, and then I wasn't. My great aunt and uncle, now brotherless, had bought my older brother a roan horse. The powdery gravel road in front of the farm house had been newly paved and the badgers were gone forever, the old single-shot shotgun leaning in old age behind the big bedroom door. A new telephone hung prominently next to the front door where the party line provided regular fare for gossip and suppertime news. I found a place next to the stale beer for my aunt's baked buns—a smell that is more than a memory. But there was a steel blue-grey jealousy, too. My brother had become my aunt's little angel, and there was no room for any other potential saints. My aunt came to see me as an instigator of every squabble, a scapegoat for every situation. I wanted to go home. But I was sent to my Grandma's, instead. She was a very stern, German-bred woman who didn't seem to like anyone, especially kids. I ate what she ate or was slapped and sent outside. I was a 10-year old boy who was ordered to play with a top and a wooden duck with leather flaps for feet— quietly... or else. Her husband was an aging carpenter who had a missing thumb and a disposition not much better than his wicked witch, I mean, wife. The only tolerable times came with Saturday and Sunday night TV. It was not allowed to watch it any other time, but I learned to totally escape into Gunsmoke, Have Gun Will Travel, The Rifleman, The Wonderful World of Disney, and Sea Hunt. The background sound of 500 Rummy still rings like the pennies in the small bowls. Sometimes my great aunt and uncle would bring my older brother to visit on Saturday night and we would get sent to a movie while the relatives played an intense game of poker. When we returned, we had to go into the living room and sit down and shut up.

I remember no move. I was back in the small town where the giant came to see me a few more times. I learned to ride a bike and blow up the neighbor's yard with an M-80. The neighborhood kids and I dammed up the street with the swiped jack-o-lanterns from many houses—much to the dismay of the county deputy who discovered the barrier first hand while a pack of cowards ran like mice in the cat's crosshairs. One day, while doing nothing in particular in the front yard, a haggard old pickup smoked down the street with a crazed collie in its wake—barking and trying to bite the tires. As it sputtered past, the dog veered up into the yard and leaped at me with zeal, took a bite of my shoulder, and continued on after the truck as if it was a regular routine. No one went to the doctor in those days.

As a parting reminder of all the memorable times, the third man endowed my mother with my youngest brother—who arrived by carriage one sunny day. He also left me with poke holes in my rear from a naily board that he swatted me with as I tried to escape up an apple tree. However questionable his methods, I quickly learned not to steal or smoke cigars.

One very important category in any writer's writings is the miscellaneous section. Although everything I have ever written might fall into this category, I have chosen to save only the works that either defy categorization or which I somehow forgot to deal with earlier. Either way, these works are likely to be of little value and even less substance—perfect fare for those among us who have developed a keen sense of apathy and a prominent nose for the wasteful things in life.

The Feeder
(2-8-96)

The feeder was left inadvertently stored
Hanging inside the garage on a cord
I doubt if the finches remembered it, though
They simply went on to the neighbor's, you know

But none of them suffered for lack of a seed
The neighbor makes sure that they get what they need
And maybe they know I've been working a lot
I certainly care, but I simply forgot

So now it's a promise I heartily make
To get out the feeder and pound in the stake
And never again will the finches fly by
Without a full belly from my neighbor and I

Small Town Folks
(3-6-96)

One nice thing about small rural towns
You have real country people—not big city clowns
With their sleek shiny shirts and their fancy fake nails
Cool cold cream women and arrogant males

Small town folks often smile and wave
And the kids seem to know how to mostly behave
City folks never make hot apple pies
Not when a five buys a burger and fries

I like to go for a long evening walk
It's a chance when my wife and I have a nice talk
While there in the city you likely get mugged
And here in the country I'll likely get hugged

But anyway, like I was saying before
I'd much rather live in a little town more
Than a rat-racy place that costs three times as much
As a big country house with an acreage and such

And one other thing that comes to my mind
I'll bet that most city folks probably find
That we in the country are boring and slow
So why are we happy—that's what I want to know

The Ache
(3-13-96)

There's an ache inside my shoes tonight
My laces might have been too tight
Or maybe I've been on my feet
Too long for them to feel too light

But soon my day will be complete
And I'll go home and take a seat
And kick my shoes off at the door
Relief at last, that can't be beat

And then my wife, who I adore
Will rub my feet and ease the sore
And tired muscles, wrong to right
I ask you, who could ask for more

Heartfelt Thoughts
(4-7-11)

With heartfelt thoughts of precious good and lasting peace
I make a new and binding covenant with my penitent self
In earnest caring and honest sharing
I swear on no good book or by no sacred soul
To give by example and a moral instinct of myself to others
To take only my due and with appreciation deeply rooted
The mirror will give credit
with practice and time well spent
The epitaph sweet with the memory of me now
The dark and fearful shadows long forgotten and forgiven
The elusive redemption found some day at last
I will do no harm anymore forever

www.ingramcontent.com/pod-product-compliance
Lightning Source LLC
LaVergne TN
LVHW021449080426
835509LV00018B/2216